The
Breakfast
Lady

To Jan
Thank you!! :)

The
Breakfast
Lady

God's Work Near and Far

Gail Fyke
2020

GAIL FYKE

XULON **PRESS**

Xulon Press
2301 Lucien Way #415
Maitland, FL 32751
407.339.4217
www.xulonpress.com

Printed in the United States of America.

ISBN-13: 9781545644638

Dedication

To the people of New Jersey, who nurtured us as one of their own.

Table of Contents

Acknowledgments

S pecial thanks to my family and friends who embraced us with love, prayers, gifts, and support from near and far. We love you and can never show enough gratitude for how you demonstrated your presence.

Special Acknowledgments:

I would like to especially recognize God's Work Near and Far in pet therapy—the St. Barnabas program in Livingston, New Jersey, and the PawPrints Ministries program in Decatur, Illinois. These programs work to bolster the spirits of those broken, ill, lonely, or depressed. My family appreciates the service that was provided to Austin in a time of dire need. We will forever believe in the power of pet therapy.

CHAPTER 1

The First Trip

March 22, 2018

Anguish grips me when I think about my text conversations with Austin on his bus ride down to Orlando with the Mt. Zion Swingsations. They were on a journey to Florida to compete in the Heart of America show choir competition—their last competition of a long, tiring season of performances. The season had been exciting and rewarding as the show choirs groups and the Combo (the instrumentation group that plays the background music for the performances) progressively mastered their shows each week. How rewarding to have their efforts culminate in a competition near the land of Disney!

This is what the fundraising had been all about throughout the school year. These are the trips that create memories that last a lifetime. How blessed are these kids to get to go so far away to compete and have fun all in one fell swoop? When I was growing up and playing in the orchestra, we were thrilled to get to play outside of the school with other kids from the area in what was known then as citywide orchestra. Any fundraising we did back in the day was to contribute to the upkeep of the program. Times have certainly changed.

Austin was texting me at home frequently with complaints of headaches. As a nurse of many years, I would text back and tell him to ask the chaperones for some pain relievers from the first aid bag that always traveled with the group. Ironically, I was usually the one dispensing these pills during our competitions but I was not able to attend the Disney trip. His headaches seemed to go away and I did not hear back from him—the activities served as great distractions. I would get an occasional picture sent to me by the chaperone parents or would see a few pictures of Austin on social media. These pictures confirmed in my mind that he was indeed having fun and these headaches were a benign problem. We got through the week and I anxiously awaited his return so I could get the firsthand recount of the fun had on the venture.

Riding on a bus for twenty hours is never an easy feat. I remember seeing the buses pulling up to the school the day they returned and watched as several of the parents disembarked, some who walked with limps after a long, tiring ride. They had clear signs of the need to slumber in their own beds that night. The kids looked exhausted too but did not get my sympathy as I thought about their resiliency and ability to rebound rapidly from sleep deprivation. They would be fine the next day. But Austin was struggling. He not only continued to have headaches, but he also had a look of someone fighting cold symptoms—congested and just feeling bad overall.

Austin returned to school for the rest of the week, pushing through his misery but finally gave me enough evidence to seek out medical attention. He seemed in clear need of an antibiotic. We stopped by the nearby Urgent Care facility where they diagnosed him with a sinus infection and placed him on antibiotics for the next ten days. Relief would be arriving soon. I felt better, Austin seemed content that we were on the right track, and life settled back into daily routines. We set our sights on getting ready for the band trip to New York City.

CHAPTER 2

The Next Trip

April 19, 2018

We congregated at the high school that afternoon, with the buses present, in anticipation of departure to New York City. It was one of those *déjà vu* moments. Hadn't I just been in this same scene in what seemed like yesterday? Kids were loading up pillows, blankets, suitcases, instruments, music, personal items, and electronic devices. Yes, another long, tiring ride on a bus was beginning. However, this time it was only fifteen hours versus the twenty-hour Orlando ride. Ha! What's the difference? Going to your destination always makes the ride seem shorter and returning always makes the ride seem longer—at least in my opinion. Austin had been at school all day except for the final focus period. The school had a policy where only three days of school time could be missed for any school trip. Since we were planning to be gone until late on April 24, we needed to start the trip later in the day. I located Austin and, much to my dismay, he had that headache-ridden appearance again. No! Not today; surely it is a tension headache or seasonal allergies headache. Yes! I made up my mind that this is late April and the pollen count must be rising. Even though the spring had been unseasonably cold, I declared seasonal allergies the culprit and moved on to picking out my seat on the bus. The band booster president, Becky, had the list of bus assignments. She had asked me if I was OK if Austin and I were on separate buses. I have always encouraged independence in my boys, so naturally, I had no issues. Plus, Austin is an extroverted person and can talk freely with whoever is around him. So, separate buses it was. I have no regrets about this decision.

Once again I got texts from Austin about his headache and once again I encouraged him to take some pain relievers from the chaperone on his bus. For some reason, my gut instinct also wanted to have some reassurance that he was not trying to get sick again so I put reinforcements in place. Austin has a tight group of band friends whom I adore. Those kids would do anything for our family and have stood the test of time with friendship. I sent a text out to all of them to keep me posted if Austin was acting weird or if they had concerns. I really didn't hear much from the group but when I sent out occasional texts checking on Austin, all seemed to be well and good. We stopped to eat dinner in eastern Indiana at a Golden Corral restaurant. When you are traveling with eighty-plus people, it is best to get in, get food, and keep going. Perfect spot! One of the chaperones on the trip had dined at this same restaurant with Boy Scout camping trips to Ohio, so he knew it was a good plan.

I think it was at this restaurant that I started to notice more symptoms in Austin. Typically, a buffet would lose money on this kid as he has a growing teenager's hearty appetite, but that night he picked at his food. Naturally, a mother thinks, "OK, did you snack too much on the bus? Did you do your bathroom business yet today? Were you too busy goofing off at dinner with your friends?" Certainly, all these scenarios have been reasons in the past for lack of interest in food. No matter the issue, we still had a great fellowship as a group that night even in a large buffet setting. I could tell by the decibel level that everyone was enjoying themselves. These are great memories that kids hold on to. Even as adults we bond together over these trips and laugh at the silliest things along the way. To me, I get the best memories from the people, the story-sharing, and pictures taken rather than the actual location we are in at the moment. I've been in what promised to be excellent places and sites before only to be disappointed or stressed out due to the masses of people. But put me in a crowd with some of these band kids or parents and a funny scene will evolve, guaranteed!

Two of the other band parents, Pam and Denise,and I were chaperoning four of the boys in the group. I am always around boys so I knew this would be a cinch. On last year's band trip, I tagged team with one other parent and chaperoned nine girls. That was a bit out of my comfort zone, but at the end of that week, I was so attached to those girls that I still call them my "adopted daughters" today. The boys I had on this trip were all known to me but not as well as Austin's closest friends. I enjoy this type of arrangement because it puts you in a unique situation where you have no choice but to get to know each other. Matt, Drake, Noah, and Ryan were the best! They sat behind me on the ride and made me smile repeatedly with their stories, laughter, quirks, and banter between each other. At one point in time in the night, I looked down and Drake had created his sleeping space on the aisle floor of the bus. He was passed out cold. As the night progressed he twisted in his sleep and now was head first in my leg space at my seat. I didn't have the heart to wake him up, so I cuddled up with my pillows against the window of the bus and tried to sleep. The keyword here is *tried*. Over the years as a nurse, I have witnessed many people sleep upright in a recliner chair due to pain or breathing problems. I will be in trouble if I ever develop those problems as I cannot sleep upright to save my life. I call my attempts at sleeping on a bus "maintenance inspections of the eyelids." Needless to say, it was a long night. We were headed to Parsippany, New Jersey, where our hotel was located. If you want to make the band trip affordable, you don't book a hotel in Manhattan. It is more economical to stay in NJ and take a bus into the city each day. Bravo to our trip coordinator, Mr. Birkey, for having the wisdom to account for that. Little did I know how much impact his decision to stay in NJ would have on Austin. God was already working....

CHAPTER 3

The Breakfast Lady

April 20, 2018

We arrived at the hotel in Parsippany at about 8:30 a.m. that Friday morning. The plan was to eat breakfast in the common area before checking into the rooms. So, enter eighty-plus people into a moderately-sized dining area. It didn't seem big enough for all of us but we made do. We weren't sure if anyone had told the hotel staff that we were coming for breakfast because they looked a bit stressed over it. I'm pretty sure someone had been told by our coordinator but sometimes the trickle down of information can get lost in translation. Excerpts from my social media post tell the story well.

> *The breakfast lady was in the dining area when we arrived. All 80 of us entered right into her space. We lined up for food and bustled about as teens do getting tables, darting for drinks and finding table service. We stressed her out and her body language looked annoyed. She even told other customers how rude the band kids were (no, we were tired and had traveled 15 hours). No one liked her, people thought she was rude and she made us a tad uneasy.*

In hindsight, she was just working hard and had her ideas on how breakfast should flow. We are Midwest people who are more laid back and not use to the "Jersey" way. Today, I know that we were just fish out of water. We got through breakfast, checked in, and then loaded up on our bus to head into the city to see the Statue of Liberty. It was a brisk morning with temperatures of only forty-five degrees. The wind was blowing off of the New York Harbor as we stood in line for what seemed forever in Battery Park, waiting for the ferry to go out to Liberty Island. Even on a cold day in April, there were hundreds of people in the park lined up to do the very same. I was trying to envision how crazy it must be in the height of tourist season in the summer. I had been that tourist back in 2001 in August. I was there on my honeymoon with Austin's dad, David, just a few short weeks before the terrorist attack on the World Trade Center. It was busy then but not miserably so. Sadly, David and I stood in line to see the statue in the very same place that became a makeshift morgue after September 11 of that same year. It was so sad to think of that scene.

Austin was not tolerating the cold. He told me several times that he was freezing. I felt his forehead and he did seem to have a fever. I wasn't sure what to do as I had no thermometer and even if I did, what were we to do without being close to the hotel or even able to access transportation easily to get there. Then out of the blue, he told me that he had lost his ticket to the Statue of Liberty. "What?" I remember raising my voice at him and questioning how that possibly could have happened just standing in line. I made him go report the incident to Mr. Birkey and fortunately he had a few extra tickets. I guess when you've chaperoned and coordinated enough of these trips like he had, you know to plan for these problems. Thank goodness for small miracles! I was dreading the thought of having to go wait in another line just to buy another ticket. After getting through security hurdles, we were finally able to get on the ferry. The wind was very brisk so I brought Austin in close to me to keep him warm as best as I could.

The question everyone had while venturing out to the statue was how far they would let us go up once inside the statue. Our tickets said pedestal on them, so I was speculating that we would only get to go that far. I was correct, as you had to pay more to get up to the crown. In past years, there was access to the torch but not anymore. You have to stop at the crown. The options that day were to ride an elevator to the observation deck of the pedestal or take the stairs. I think I had too much coffee that morning as I somehow thought I could master the stairs. Ha! Fortunately, as I suffered through the ascent, others not too much younger than me paused to rest and self- resuscitate as well. Misery loves company! We laughed at ourselves and finally reached the observation area. Austin fared well with the stairs and actually enjoyed making fun of my efforts. Yes, we actually had a few laughs in the middle of our trials and tribulations. We did a quick view from the deck and headed back down. The kids did a group picture on Liberty Island and then we headed back so as not to miss the last ferry that fit our schedule.

We split into our chaperoned groups for dinner. The boys in my group picked out an upscale pizza restaurant but I spent so much time on the cell phone that I missed out on the fellowship for the most part. You see, I was making calls trying to get a prescription for more sinus-infection antibiotics from my physician connections back home in Illinois. I was now convinced that the sinus infection had returned and if Austin could just get back on the antibiotics, maybe we could rebound a bit and enjoy this trip. I successfully made that happen and after going through a few hoops, got a prescription from a pharmacy in the Times Square vicinity. This was not what I thought I would be doing while in New York City amid thousands of tourists. Austin took a dose of it right on the spot and in my mind we were sailing again. We headed to the Empire State building and did a quick climb to the top for an awesome view of the city. Then, the bus headed back to Parsippany. It was a long day for sure, but, as it turned out, an even longer night for Austin.

CHAPTER 4

Breakfast Lady Round Two

April 21, 2018

I found Austin unmotivated the next morning to go to breakfast. He had thrown up in the night on his blanket that he had brought from home. He didn't feel up to much and he was not going to go into the city with the group. Basically, he had decided to stay in bed for the day and skip the planned activities. All he wanted me to get him from the breakfast buffet was grapes and watermelon. I looked at him, in a quandary. What was going on? Was he dehydrated and thus lacking energy? Was he low on calories from not eating since Thursday? Who craves watermelon in April?? I was baffled by what was in front of me. Maybe it would be good to let him get some sleep and then he would feel better. I was grabbing at straws. I was away from home and caught up in the flurry of kids around me and simply struggling to help my son. The best nurse in me was out of solutions. If he was throwing up, how could I get more antibiotics in him? All I wanted to do was drive home and call this trip over. But I had no vehicle and I still had hope that a day of rest would help. Plus, he kept insisting that he wanted to go to the *Phantom of the Opera* that night. He thought we could take an Uber into the city later and join the group. So, that was our plan. After breakfast, I decided to ask Breakfast

Lady if she had any grapes that I could have to take to the room. As I attempted the question, she looked at me hastily and said in her thick Jersey accent "Walk and talk! Walk and talk!" So I chased behind her to the kitchen and she handed me a bowl of grapes. Mission accomplished!

I ran into Breakfast Lady before I headed to the room. My post pertaining to this moment:

> *I didn't get to go on the day activities because Austin was sick and stayed in bed. I went to breakfast without him and saw her and decided to put a plug in for our kids. I thanked her for putting up with a big group from the day before and then told her how awesome the kids are and musically gifted. She softened.....basically it's called kill em with kindness. We chatted for another minute and parted ways.*

As Austin slept, I decided to check on my lunch options. The hotel had a few items for sale that I could microwave but I was in the mood for more than just soup or microwaved macaroni and cheese. I learned that the closest food was a mile down the road so I set out on foot to explore. The temperatures were better that day than they were at the statue experience. I think it was high fifties or low sixties, just perfect for a hike. I cut through business parking lots as I walked along the busy highway. Finally, a Fuddruckers appeared and lunch was on the horizon! When you dine by yourself it's basically a people-watching event. You can play on your cell phone to look busy but I prefer to people-watch. A young couple walked by me so I gathered up the gumption to ask them about the best way to ride into the city for the *Phantom* show. They gave me a brief overview of the Uber vs. Lyft rides and even helped me download the Lyft app. By the time we parted ways, they had helped me figure out the most affordable option. Nice people! I finished lunch and then thought about the long walk back to the hotel. For a fleeting moment, I decided if I saw a nice elderly couple leaving that I would ask for a ride to the hotel. This would make me feel like less of a hitchhiker—you know, tell them about your kid being sick and plead your case on how far you had to walk. Of course, no one fitting that description was leaving, so on foot I went. It was much less walking than I would have done in the city. Back at the hotel, I checked on Austin and then scooped up his blanket to take it to the laundry area within the hotel. I passed the time waiting on the machines by watching the funeral procession for Barbara Bush. The television in the fitness room was close by so I tuned in. I never have time to watch TV at home or keep up on current events. Life goes so fast and is so hectic sometimes that the world goes on and one can become oblivious to it. I was on that roller-coaster but God gave me a few moments to slow down and just breathe. It would be the first of many opportunities to just slow down. I truly believe that when you are on the fast track of life that you need to intentionally create the pauses now and then just to breathe and reflect on the simple things. So, the laundry and fitness rooms were my pause for the day. And I said a prayer for the Bush family.

Austin insisted that we go into the city to see the *Phantom of the Opera* on Broadway. He had been waiting for months for this show. He had watched the movie to get a feel for the plot and the band had been rehearsing a medley from the *Phantom* soundtrack, which they were to play aboard the USS *Intrepid* at the Intrepid Sea, Air & Space Museum in NYC on Monday, April 23. Additionally, he had been listening to the soundtrack at times and really enjoyed the music. So, I decided to go with the Uber option that the young couple at the restaurant had helped me map out. It seemed easier than the Lyft system. Not realizing that they would be arriving so fast after my request I hurried Austin along and told him I would meet him in the hotel lobby. Six minutes later, my driver arrived but there was no sign of Austin. I called him and urged him to get down to the lobby immediately. I then went to the room only to find him not dressed for the evening and moving at a snail's pace. Frustration! I ran down to apologize to the driver and a few minutes later Austin showed up in the lobby. I immediately learned that Uber drivers charge waiting fees, which we so deservingly earned in that moment. It wasn't like Austin to act like this. He is a people-pleaser and I had a growing sense that his ailments were getting worse. I asked him if he wanted to stay home and he declined. I reassured him that all we had to do was sit and watch a show and ride the bus home. He was fine with that idea. We ended up enjoying the ride into the city and laughing over silly things. We made the decision to stop by the Nintendo store first, since he had missed out on his group going there earlier in the day. I was worried with the congestion of traffic that we wouldn't have time to do this but our driver was an expert at the traffic and got us to the store with plenty of time to browse and still get to the theater in time.

Austin walked like a turtle in the store so I pushed him along and found a sweatshirt that I thought he would like. His indifference to anything I was saying led me to discern that we should just head to the show. He could not have cared less about anything in the Nintendo store, another sign that he wasn't acting right. So, we set out on foot with our phone navigation systems to find the theater. I remember arguing with him because we both had our phones out and my directions were different from his. I naturally thought he was wrong because of how he had been acting but ultimately, I let him have his way and fortunately we found the band group with time to spare. The seats were excellent and the kids were excited in anticipation of the performance.

This was my second time seeing the *Phantom of the Opera* but I was just as excited as well. The opening scene with the auction commenced and all eyes were fixed on the stage. All but Austin's—I looked over and he was sleeping! No, not already! I nudged him and he woke for a few minutes and nodded back off to sleep. All I could do was leave him alone and get through the show.

At intermission time, he had to use the restroom so I went with him and waited outside of the men's room. There was a long line even for the men's room but I waited patiently as

Austin inched his way up to the door and proceeded inside. I waited for another ten minutes and finally asked one of Austin's peers to go in and tell him to hurry. I waited to no avail. Finally, after all the patrons had returned to the theater I started to panic. Should I go in the men's room? The thought of it was tempting but it also seemed awkward for fear other males were still in there. To my relief, Mr. Birkey came off the stairs and was heading into the bathroom. I asked for help and he was able to move Austin along. He found him in a stall and insisted that he hurry and get back into the show. To this day, I will swear that Austin was sleeping in there but I haven't pressed the issue with him. We got through the second half of the night and loaded up on the bus and headed to the hotel. I was told later that Austin threw up in the garbage can in the lobby of the hotel. In hindsight, at least it was at the hotel and not in the middle of the *Phantom* performance. Either way, his system was sending out signals for help and I was soon going to really be hearing them.

CHAPTER 5

Where Would I Be Without the Breakfast Lady?

April 22, 2018

The next morning, I woke up early in order to get cleaned up and check on Austin. He had several doses of the new antibiotic in him and maybe I would see signs of improvement. Not the case—he was even more tired and sluggish-acting than the night before. I found him in his bed in the same clothes he had worn the day before, sleeping on top of grapes and animal crackers that Becky had given him before bed. I was seriously at a point where I was ready to just put him in a rental car and drive back to Illinois for medical attention. He had gone too many days without food and water and I was sure he was getting more dehydrated. I asked one of the parents, Brian, to try to help get Austin into the shower and motivated to at least make an attempt to go on the bus and just slowly move about the city today at our own pace. No schedules, no commitments to do anything with the group, just he and I going at our own pace. The bus was about to leave and Brian was able to get him to shower but then he just wanted to be in bed. So, I opted out of the city experience and sat in my room in silence as Austin slept. I just sat there in a quandary as to what to do next.

Here we were, in a faraway place with no car, no familiarity with healthcare facilities, and not a lot of money outside of expected trip expenses. In my mind, I thought maybe we could go to a hospital and get IV fluids and he would perk up and we could just stay at the hotel until Tuesday, when the bus would be heading back to Illinois. I started to sob, not knowing what to do next. I rarely struggle with figuring out situations. I have always been known to be that resource person that others turn to in times of uncertainty. Usually, I come up with some kind of plan, but not today. In these moments, I turn to God and I ask for help. He has never failed me. He is always with me, but sometimes I forget and worry unnecessarily.

That was it—I needed to take action and get my son help. I ran down to the front desk and asked the two ladies standing there to find me a rental car business in Parsippany so that I could drive back to Illinois. They looked at me hesitantly and wondered why I was departing from the band group. Now I started sobbing again and tried to explain that Austin was very sick and needed medical attention. I told them, "I'm a nurse and I have people back in Illinois that I want to take care of him." Again, they looked bewildered about why I would do such a crazy thing. Clearly, the lady that picked up the phone and started looking for rental cars was the manager. She seemed to have an in-charge person demeanor. The other staff person was very quiet and stood there passively as the manager tried her best to help me. Then out of nowhere, Breakfast Lady approached me. She had overheard the demands I was making. Here is the post:

> *I insisted the manager find me a rental car place as I wept about my son being sick and needing to go back to Illinois. Enter Breakfast Lady onto the scene overhearing my commands. She got in my face with her Jersey accent and demanded I take him to the local hospital NOW and that she'd be driving me there herself. The manager then told me all local rental car places were closed on*

*Sundays. Breakfast lady got her keys out and said
"Let's go.....get your son."*

Well, I was a bit scared of her, to be honest. She was barely
five feet tall but her personality was larger than that. I snapped
back to reality and succumbed to her plan and went to get
Austin. I grabbed our bathroom bags and a couple small items
and we headed to the lobby. The manager was not willing to
let an off-the-clock employee drive us, so she had the shuttle
guy take us to St. Clare's Hospital in Denville, NJ. They all reassured us that St. Clare's was a hospital with a good reputation
and very short wait times in their Emergency Room. So, off
we went. Our driver spoke very little English and seemed to
be lost trying to find the hospital. I would see the big *H* signs
go by but he would miss the turns. I made many gestures and
somehow we found our way. The next hurdle was a road race
going on with police cars blocking the way to the hospital. We
were in a shuttle bus, not an ambulance, so we were held at
bay. My panic mode was now coming back to the surface and I
was ready to jump out of the shuttle to ask the police for help
myself but I finally got through to my non-English-speaking
driver to roll down the window and summon the police officer
to our vehicle. I screamed out the window that my son needed
the hospital immediately and BOOM ,we were allowed through.
He dropped us off and we headed to triage. I had a gut feeling
as we arrived that I should have brought all the luggage....

CHAPTER 6

If I Can't Have Illinois, Give Me New York

T he hotel people were right. We had virtually no wait in this Emergency Room in Denville, NJ. I would later learn that this hospital was known for their psychiatric services. A host of patients came in while we were there, needing that service. I felt sad for them. Amazingly, the staff handled them calmly and did not get escalated with them. This is why I am not an ER nurse—they see it all and deal with so many curve balls. We were inundated during our visit with lab draws, information-sharing, x-rays, and IV bags. Austin had a low-grade fever but all of his tests were coming back with minimal findings:

> *Dehydration being worked on, appendicitis ruled out, spinal tap next looking for cause of his lethargy, need to check for what's called myeloencephalitis which is possible after having had recent stomach bug (which he had a few weeks ago). Oh how I wish I was home with my team of colleagues. This is scary!*

Sometimes I balk at the fact that we have to follow so many protocols in healthcare. To me, it feels like using a recipe, but evidence-based practice requires we use protocols for safety purposes and to make sure we all follow best practices as determined by the published research. That day, I was blessed to have a protocol in place in the Interventional Radiology department. Before any spinal tap when a patient is having cognition changes, their protocol required a CT of the head. So, off we went to have that done. I anxiously waited outside of the door of the room that Austin was in. Minutes later, the radiologist steps out to talk to me and proclaimed in his robust Jersey voice that he had found the problem and there would be no need for a spinal tap. He took me to the images and showed me his findings. My heart sank; right there for anyone to see was clear evidence of what he told me was a brain abscess. He added that they do these CTs of the head first before spinal taps for this very reason—just in case there is a problem in the brain. He would have caused more problems to Austin's system had he performed that procedure. Now my brain was messed up too. What does all this mean? What is the treatment? Can we go back to Illinois now? What needs to be done? I was numb, and standing in what felt like a foreign land. I wanted to run, hit something, scream at the radiologist for finding this problem, scream at him also for being so excited that he found the problem, curse out loud, and yes, I even wanted to question God why He was doing this to my son. I had about every emotion one could have all within the five minutes that I had to process this news. As we headed back to the ER, I was grateful that Austin was so out of it that he didn't hear the radiologist talk about his findings. I would have to find the way to tell him. I would be the one to share this with him. But for now, I had to call his dad and break it to him and ask for him to come to the bedside.

I didn't even have to say more than a couple of sentences for David to declare he was on his way. Miraculously, he worked it out for our other son Jamie to be able to stay at his best friend's house so that he could head to New Jersey. He found arrangements for his dog and got his belongings in order. He tried to find a plane ticket but there were only tickets for the next day and he wanted to head towards his son right away without delay. Together, we made a plan to have him pick up my van and drive it to New Jersey. It would be a fifteen-hour drive but Austin was worth the pain and agony of having to do the drive. He set out fueled by sheer adrenaline.

Now came the discussion with the ER physician on where to get this brain abscess treated. He shared with me that Austin would definitely need to be transferred to a center where a pediatric neurosurgeon and pediatric ENT surgeon could work together to surgically clean out the abscess. He knew of several options in the area but needed to make some calls first. I said to him "Surely, you're sending us to New York?" He looked at me oddly and in a puzzled sort of way and responded, "No, we don't need New York, we've got you covered right here in Jersey." And then he walked away. I didn't know if I offended him or the state of New Jersey. It was not my intention. I just thought New York was the mecca for complex problems such as ours, and they would be the only ones to figure out in this region. I didn't know what I didn't know. He came back after an hour and a half of phone calls and told me that St. Barnabas in Livingston, NJ, just about twenty minutes away was going to take us in and the surgeons had accepted the case. I had originally been told that surgery would be later that night but due to the surgeons needing to coordinate their schedules to work on Austin within the same afternoon, they planned the surgery for 2 p.m. the next day. For now, we just needed to get moved to St. Barnabas. I now knew that I had better get my family briefed and try to respond to all the text messages from the band director, parents, and close friends of Austin from the trip. I was exhausted by this point, with information overload from the day, having to watch over Austin, wiping away tears, and having to make rapid decisions.

I have been blessed with so many family and friends reaching out for us today with prayers and concerns and offerings to help and I am overwhelmed by your love. Thank you because Austin and I and his dad feel your presence. Due to exhaustion and sleep deprivation and needing to be attuned to the bedside, I will post progress as we go but will be limited on responses but know that I know you are all there and so does Austin. His dad is starting a 15 hour trek by van up here by himself tonight so pray for him too. We go into surgery tomorrow with an expert neurosurgery and ENT team and clean out the abscess on the right frontal side of the outer brain. They expect him to do well. Austin knows the plan and is being a trooper, very brave.

Somewhere in all the flurry of activities I had held Austin's hand and asked him to listen as I explained the diagnosis to him. He was so lethargic that I don't think he truly understood. He would wake up off and on but basically slept. He knew when he had to use the bathroom and he always answered all the questions correctly for the staff, so that was a blessing. He never lost his faculties even with this monster infection in his head. He had even talked briefly on the phone to his dad and brother somewhere in the day and told them he loved them. It was heartwarming, in a way, that in the middle of hardship, the two brothers could set their differences aside and come together. Soon, the ambulance team arrived to take us to St. Barnabas and off we went.

I will forever be indebted to this small hospital in Denville, NJ, for finding the problem, but better yet, I will always remember how the breakfast lady in Parsippany saved his life and how the most unlikely people in your life, the people you may not like or have had challenging encounters with, could be the people that you need help from some day. You see, if I had driven Austin home to Illinois I would have put him at risk of having his infection cause severe repercussions and horrible outcomes. Breakfast lady pushed me to access care rapidly and thank God I did. Even if you don't connect with someone, kill 'em with kindness, kill 'em with kindness....

CHAPTER 7

First Impressions of St. Barnabas

We arrived quickly at St. Barnabas. The building was all lit up in green fluorescent lights and looked like a building that would easily blend in with lights of the Las Vegas strip. I thought it looked kind of interesting. It looked modern and much bigger than the last hospital. I asked immediately how many beds the hospital had and I was told close to 600—not as many as I had surmised. We were taken directly to the Pediatric Intensive Care Unit on the fourth floor. I remember walking down the hallway with the paramedics and Austin on the stretcher. Would they be welcoming? Would they look caring? Or would they be annoyed about another admission coming and more work to do? We couldn't have been more welcomed. Austin's team had the room ready and greeted him within minutes of arrival with body language that looked very accepting. I have to add that it was near the end of their twelve-hour shift when we arrived yet I didn't see fatigue written all over their faces. Thank goodness! First impressions were going well! We spent the next couple of hours telling our story about a band trip gone bad for this Illinois family and why we were in this area, and made sure everyone knew that we were not from Chicago. When you are far away from home and you tell people you are from Illinois, they automatically assume you are from the Chicago area. I have lived in Central Illinois all my life and have a deep love for my community. People back home had bonded together to support our family through this illness. Geographically my community is a quick drive to Chicago but my goal was to acknowledge the strength of my home town and to give them their own identity. I started my geography lesson with them from the start and explained that there are cities below Interstate 80 in Illinois. I love my Chicago friends dearly but I'm just being truthful about perceptions.

I noticed that several physicians were stopping by our room. There were pediatric intensivists and pediatricians. I would soon learn that there was a pediatric intensivist available at all times for whatever the needs of the patient and families were. We had one of their names on our whiteboard in our room at all times. This group of providers was the best. I have hospitalists and intensivists back at my home hospital as well but I had not had the experience of being in the customer shoes at this capacity. It was reassuring to know that a physician was only a small distance from the bedside. Our room was comfortable and when I informed the team that I had no lodging, and for the time being only a bathroom bag and the clothes on my back, they kicked into high gear. They gave me a family sleeping room down the hall and showed me a shower I could access and a small pantry that I could use. There was also a little food area in their nurse's station where I was welcome to grab coffee, bagels, and muffins from any time I wanted. I looked at them and asked, "You will let me in your nurse's station?" They said of course.

It felt weird to be able to be in the same space with the people caring for Austin like I was crossing the boundary line. But they never minded, and anytime I needed someone they encouraged us to reach out or just step into the station. Wow, how inviting. I made sure to not abuse this privilege because I know firsthand how busy healthcare staff can be. To know that we were welcome was such a good feeling. Austin got settled in for the night and I retreated to the sleeping room to try to get a few hours of sleep. I checked in with David to see how the drive was going, and updated my family, the band director, and other key people about the new hospital. I had to smile when they shared that they had already been researching St. Barnabas on the internet and I was in an excellent hospital. In fact, it was the first time that I was told by people that God put us in that place. We were in excellent hands.

St. Barnabas Medical Center at night

CHAPTER 8

Day of Surgery

April 23, 2018

We were awakened early by the surgeons wanting to come by and introduce themselves plus give us information about what to expect from the surgery. They were very thorough and seemed so confident. I felt a huge presence within both of our lead surgeons. I'm sure they had great reputations and only did complicated cases, for the most part. I call them our lead surgeons because each surgeon had a team of five to eight resident physicians with them on any given day. We were in a huge teaching institution and it was very clear that Austin's surgeons were great educators. My post for that morning:

> *The night went well for Austin (getting a little grumpy but that's to be expected). Surgeons all came this morning—2 leads and about 8 surgery residents. We are on for about 2pm-2:30p. They anticipate 2-3 weeks here in NJ and hopefully a transfer of follow up care to experts closer to home. Thank you for all the prayers!*

Today would have been the day that Austin was going to be playing with the Mt. Zion band aboard the USS *Intrepid* in

New York City. I was at his bedside having a moment of sadness about both of us missing this experience when my cell phone lit up with a notification "Melissa is live in New York, NY." Oh, how wonderful! I jumped out of my chair and basically shouted at Austin that the band was getting ready to perform on the *Intrepid*. He opened his eyes and smiled and gave me enough of a response to reassure me that he knew what that meant. I put the phone to his ear so that he could hear the performance. In my mind, I felt like I could count it as part of his preoperative regimen. Music was piping into his head as he lay in the hospital bed waiting for one of the most profound events of his life. Music—it is one of the best therapies that I can recommend. I also told Austin how everyone was praying for him and sending love. His groggy response: "I don't deserve it."

I was getting a bit worried that David would be too late to see Austin before surgery. I had checked in with him several times on his progress but there was no guarantee. Even though surgery was scheduled for 2 p.m., I knew from my years of nursing that patients were taken down to the preoperative area much sooner than the surgery start time. I decided to ask the nurses if it would be possible to let us stay with Austin in the preoperative phase and then say goodbye as he needed to go into the surgery suite. Without hesitation, they told me, "Of course!" Phew! I was beginning to realize that this hospital was user-friendly as they say. I started to let down some of the roadblocks in my head that one can create when in a new environment, trying to establish first impressions. Wouldn't life be so much easier if our minds didn't work like that? First impressions can be lasting and can lock out all the great characteristics we all bring to the table. To walk into a situation with an open mind and to think about how everyone came to work today with the intention of providing the best care that they can—how would this change work environments not only at hospitals but in restaurants, banks, or any service related businesses? Yes, I think it was at this minute that I decided I could be a mom for Austin instead of a nurse trying to double check everyone's work. The Barnabas team HAD this; it was so comforting for my soul.

I have to start talking about our favorite nurse Paige now. She was our first day-shift nurse that we were assigned to. She was very energetic and personable. Austin liked her immediately. As part of the assessment of a patient with a neurologic problem, the nursing staff has to perform what is called neuro checks. They look at pupils, grip strength, movement of arms and legs, and much more. It is also imperative to check to see if the patient knows what year it is, what location they are at, who the President is, and who people in the room are. Paige decided to take things to a new level and quiz Austin on what her name was every time and for him to say it loud and proud. If he mumbled her name then she would make him say it again. If it was too soft, she would make him say it louder. It became the game. I loved her approach. She also declared to Austin that she was the prettiest nurse in their department (another tactic to make him remember her—hey, it worked!). He was so lethargic that he could barely open his eyes to see her; I think she had to pry them open at times. But, by gosh he was going to remember her no matter if he could see or not!

Austin with Paige

Luck was on our side (or you could say a higher power), and David walked into Austin's room about a half hour before they took Austin down to surgery. It was a tearful reunion and Austin was happy to see him. He disclosed to everyone that he drove the fifteen hours straight only stopping for gas and bathroom breaks. And now, he had been up for forty hours but the adrenaline was enough to power him through. Surely there would be time for a nap later, maybe? How does one sleep when your child is having brain surgery? I suspected at that moment that he would be up a lot longer. Time would tell. The transporter arrived at the bedside ready to take Austin away. It wasn't a good feeling for either one of us. I actually experienced a sense of numbness to the situation. It's like it really wasn't happening and I was ready to wake up from the nightmare.

CHAPTER 9

Off to Surgery

April 23, 2018 Continued

We sat by Austin's stretcher in the preoperative department as the staff bustled around getting other patients
ready for surgery. Austin, of course, mostly slept but we tried to
give him words of encouragement that we would be right there
when he woke back up, that he was going to do fine, that he was
in good hands. The anesthesiologist stopped by to discuss his
end of the care. He shared the need to keep Austin on a ventilator after surgery for just for a short-term period as a strategy
to let his brain rest. The plan was to be on the vent overnight
with a goal of getting the tube out the day after surgery. I had
seen this done many times back home so I explained it a little
more to David and we were fine with the plan. Soon thereafter,
the anesthesia team was ready to start the case and needed
Austin moved back to the surgery suite. We gave out hugs and
kisses and said our "see you laters" and off he went.

It was devastating, watching the stretcher carrying Austin
leave us. David and I were both sobbing and I felt like I had
just sent my son to war. I looked at his perfect little head and
all his hair and thought about how it would be changed when
he got back. He came into the world with ten little fingers and
ten little toes and a head intact. Babies are born with different

shapes and sizes of heads but generally, the skull is fully present and intact. We take it for granted. Ultrasounds give us information to prep us for how our babies will present when they enter the world. Some have birth defects and families take steps to manage what is necessary, but for the most part, we expect a normal head that will last a life time. So, you have to change your vision based on reality. I knew I would continue to love Austin unconditionally no matter what the circumstances are. And, he would be the same person no matter how this surgery altered him—beautiful inside and out.

Knowing that I only had a narrow window to get back to the hotel in Parsippany to retrieve our luggage, I scooted out immediately with the van and headed in that direction. David stayed behind to make sure a parent was available if surgery staff had any concerns or questions. The band families had been kind and had packed up our personal belongings and took the suitcases down to the front desk in anticipation of me coming by. The drive to the hotel caused a sense of sadness in me as I thought about having been in the ambulance the last time we were on these roads. It was a short fifteen-minute drive and I quickly ran into the hotel, where the staff let me do one last walk-through of the rooms for missed items and then headed back to the hospital.

The parents had informed me that they had put an envelope in the front of my suitcase with some donations that they had collected the night before. I found cards in there for Austin that they had all signed as well. The generosity that was in that envelope spoke volumes of the love and support of the band families. They gave us enough to know that we were going to be able to make it in New Jersey for the days to come. I was deeply touched and humbled and just sat in the van and sobbed even more. It made me feel blessed to be part of such a cohesive group that would go to such lengths to promote our welfare. The compassion demonstrated through those gifts will live within me forever.

Many things transpired while we were in the hospital that were told to me later by involved parties. As I sent text after text to the band director throughout the day that we headed to the hospital, he had to make the decision on how to tell the kids what was happening to Austin. He knew it would be difficult and very emotional to hear but he felt the onus to keep them informed and to solicit their support. After returning to the hotel the night before Austin's surgery, he pulled the kids and chaperones together in the lobby of the hotel at 11:30 p.m. and disclosed the updates. He told them of Austin's diagnosis and how surgery was scheduled for the next day. I'm not exactly sure what was said next but many have told me that it was a somber moment.

CHAPTER 10

When Life Hands You Lemons

April 23, 2018 Continued

Austin was in surgery until approximately 10 p.m. that night. It was a very long day, waiting for him to return, but we knew that his problems were complex and needed intricate attention. I made a decision as the day progressed to do Facebook updates instead of trying to keep up with phone calls and texts. There were too many people who wanted to know Austin's progress, so I felt that it would free up my time needed at the bedside to blast regular posts for everyone. Plus, if the information came from me to the masses then there would be no room for translation snafus. I wanted people back home to have the accurate story of what was really happening with Austin.

Both surgeons came up to Austin's room before he was brought back to give us feedback from surgery. The first to arrive was the head and neck surgeon, Dr. Lin. He described the sinuses in detail and reassured us that he had completely cleaned out the right side and that the left side was clear. He spoke with confidence that everything had gone well and that he would like to go in again in about a week and do another sinus cleansing, which was usual and customary after this type of surgery. He proclaimed that the procedure he performed on Austin should relieve him from ever having a sinus infection again. One thing that surprised David and I was the discovery that Austin had a deviated septum, found during surgery. We didn't know Austin had a displaced nasal septum. To us, his nose looked just fine. Dr. Lin stated that he was probably born with it as many people are and just never had any problems but straightening it would contribute to better outcomes for Austin.

Several hours later, the neurosurgeon came to the room to debrief with us on his findings. I don't think I was emotionally prepared for his news. He spoke in a very somber tone and I could tell he was trying not to upset us. There was an overwhelming amount of infection in the right side of Austin's brain. Not only were the epidural and subdural spaces affected but also the deep brain tissue. They had to remove a large flap from the skull in order to get to the part of the brain that needed to be cleansed. The bone was sent to pathology for analysis but was probably contaminated with infection as well. He felt confident that he had cleansed as much of the infection as possible out from the site but was unable to manipulate the deep brain tissue due to the risk involved. He glanced at us with a look that I'll never forget and said: "We will have to leave that area up to antibiotics and prayers." He genuinely felt that Austin had a good prognosis because of early interventions but he also had grave concerns that there was ischemic (reduction of blood flow to parts of the brain) areas caused by the infection and we could possibly see stroke-like effects after Austin wakes up. We were warned that Austin may be disoriented for a period of time, not recognize us, have weakness on his left side, and may need rehabilitation for several weeks to regain strength and baseline functioning. He also mentioned that he would need to go back into surgery in a week to do more cleansing of the brain. For now, he was going to leave Austin on the ventilator overnight and try to get him to breathe on his own tomorrow. And then he left. Wow, how to digest all this information; my head was spinning and my stomach upset. I don't remember if I cried or not. I think David and I just rehashed what we thought we had heard and sat quietly, waiting for Austin's return. I had a hard time getting my arms around the whole idea that this was really happening. It just seemed too insane and intangible in a sense. The optimist in me was struggling to see any positive at all in such grim circumstances. Life was unfair right now. Austin didn't deserve this right in the height of his high school years. Why, why, why? My post from that night:

> *Surgery complete! Austin came through a tough procedure and both surgeons are satisfied with how he did. He will be on the ventilator overnight and hopefully off tomorrow. They cleaned out the abscess and left off the skull flap so they can rinse the area again briefly next week. Sinuses cleaned and nasal septum straightened. Lots of brain swelling we are told and not to expect his cognition to be intact right away.....maybe a few days down the road. He will have the bone replaced to his skull in 3 months. I am pushing to go home in a few weeks, do IV antibiotics at home for a few weeks more after that and vie for Chicago experts to put bone back in place. This was all due to invasive sinusitis. Thank you so much for staying with us all day. Will be a rough go for a few days.*

I found an ounce of optimism as soon as Austin rolled in from surgery. I remember saying to David how good he looked compared to what I had contrived in my mind. I was expecting more facial disfigurement and more swelling than was present. He seemed to be doing well on the ventilator and didn't have a cluster of tubes and lines like I had imagined. Half of his head was shaved but I didn't see the incision line immediately because I was sitting to his left side. I guess a slow introduction to the surgical site was a benefit. Immediately, I set my mind on how the worst was over and now we could focus on recovery. I made up my mind right away that the power of prayers and positivity would be the formula for healing. Making lemonade from lemons? Where would it get us to grieve over the situation? Why should we focus on the *what if's,* or all the possibilities that could go wrong? God would navigate the plan that He had created. God would hold us and get us through and we could be at peace with that notion. Yes, God is good and good things will come from all of this. Everything happens for a reason, I would just have to look for the signs.

Sign At Head of Bed After Surgery

We were weary and had not eaten dinner, but we wanted to stay with Austin for as long as we could. He was heavily sedated but at times he would move his hand up to his endotracheal tube (breathing tube) and try to pull it out. We would grab his hand and urgently call the nurse. John was on for the night and we immediately became connected with him. He was very caring and easy to talk to. Anything we needed, John was on it. I felt comfortable knowing that he would take care of Austin all night. John gave additional doses of sedation to offset Austin's efforts to extubate himself. I imagine any one of us would be the same way if we had an irritating tube down our throat. I finally caved in to the thought of sleep and said good night to Austin and headed to my sleeping room. David was hesitant to leave for fear that the tube would be pulled out so he stayed in the chair intending to be there all night. John insisted that he get some sleep but David stayed awake. He was now going on fifty hours without sleep. Surely, he would just pass out from exhaustion....

CHAPTER 11

Day after Surgery

April 24, 2018

t was a restless night. The thought of Austin going through all this catastrophic illness just worried me. I wanted so much to trade places with him and give him his life back. Parents shouldn't have to watch their child go through brain surgery and be dependent on a breathing apparatus. He should be getting on a bus today in Parsippany, NJ, and heading back to Mt. Zion, IL. He should be giggling with his friends and talking about newly-created memories. I should be on the other bus exhausted from having walked all over New York City yet exhilarated from the fellowship.

Both teams of surgeons with their residents made early rounds that day so David was present for the updates and I joined in shortly after. The plan was to have an MRI as a routine follow-up after surgery and to try to get off the ventilator if the MRI results were acceptable. Austin had a pretty good night. John had finally convinced David to go to sleep by telling him "It's my job to keep him safe. I'll stay in the room and watch his hands so you can sleep." What an awesome nurse! How comforting those words were to David. Sometimes it's all in how you connect with the families that makes all the difference.

Establishing that trust is key and we felt like we were beginning to trust in the Barnabas staff. They told us everything they were doing as they performed the tasks. In my experience, it is called "narrative care." It left us with no questions on what was going on and what would be happening next. We headed into another PICU Grand Rounds at 9 a.m. This meant that every day while Austin was there, they would have the nurse assigned to him give a report to a multidisciplinary team who would contribute to the care plan for the day.

Discharge planning was always addressed too, as that was our ultimate goal. I made sure to tell the team that day that our number one goal, outside of Austin progressing, was to get us back to Illinois as fast as possible because our twelve-year-old son, Jamie, was staying at a friend's house until our return. They completely understood and promised that they would try to set up care in Chicago or St. Louis so we could achieve that goal. I was impressed that the team included ancillary staff from areas such as dietary, respiratory, child life coordination, case management, social services, and the pediatric intensivist physicians. They were able to update orders and let David and I contribute during the rounds all in one fell swoop. It was my favorite part of the day, getting to know what to expect!

Not all the news in Grand Rounds is what you want to hear, however. Clearly, from my post, this was one of those times:

> *Through tears I type this update as I sit in the MRI waiting room. We were told this morning that Austin will need inpatient Rehab at a children's facility in St. Louis or Chicago after leaving here. His brain has been impacted much like a stroke and he is expected to have gait and balance problems for some time. Still need to wait and see day by day. He is still on vent until later. He was not moving his left side this morning but they did a small "sedation vacation" and his left side started kicking and swinging so thank God for that. His left eye was open and moving around. I was telling the staff that he probably wouldn't get that driver's license as planned for July and that is when the eye went crazy. Maybe he can hear me....this is just awful and David and I can't stop crying.*

The investigation of which city to pick—Chicago or St. Louis—ensued. There were pros and cons for both locations but ultimately, it had to work for us and had to work with the physicians who would be doing the handoffs of care to their colleagues in their respective fields. We had been assigned an infectious disease specialist along with the other physicians on the team. Her name was Dr. Hasan and we liked her from the minute we met her. She was popular with the nurses and, actually, I didn't meet a staff person the whole time we were there that didn't have the highest respect for her as well as loads of compliments. I completely understood why as time marched on. She decided on this day that she would help to find us the neurosurgeon and infectious disease specialist we would need back in Illinois. She had many Chicago connections as she had done a fellowship at Lurie's Children's Hospital. She would check on her resources and get back to us. I was delighted that she had spent time in Chicago! This would make things potentially easier for us with arrangements. We weren't ruling out St. Louis yet because we knew they had a great reputation and one of our neighbors had been hospitalized there with amazing outcomes after a stroke. Again, children should not have to go through such horrible problems such as stroke or brain abscess but surely down the road, it makes them resilient.

The child life coordinator, Laura, came by again this day. This time, I had complied with requests that she made when Austin was admitted, and she had been patiently waiting. I finally emailed her some pictures of Austin so that she could enlarge them and hang them on his walls. Not only did she print them and enlarge them, but she also laminated them; we were so touched. Austin was still sedated but we decorated the room anyway, to surprise him when he woke up. We tried to showcase his music passion by using a lot of band pictures and show choir competition photos where he was in the Combo group that played instruments onstage while the show choir groups perform. I took pictures of the walls of his room and posted them for friends and family back home to see. I wanted them to know that they were important in Austin's life and these pictures would serve as a source of inspiration for Austin to get better and get back home.

Laura was awesome to work with. Her job was to work with pediatric patients during their hospitalization to keep them active, busy, and focused on wellness and distraction instead of illness. She offered many things while we were there. It really depends on what your child's interests are, how old your child is, and how the child is feeling. She was incredibly flexible working with us. We enjoyed hearing her stories about being from New York and marrying a New Jersey boy and how she had to adapt. It was really the first time I started getting an education on the "Jersey way."

One of the other things Laura did for us was to introduce the Make- A- Wish program to us. At first, when she brought it up I was taken aback because I thought the program was only for terminally-ill children. When she saw the frightened look on my face, she immediately waved her hands in the air and declared, "No! No! Your son isn't terminal. The program is also for kids with life-threatening illnesses. I just have to sign him up for it while he is in the middle of his critical days in order to qualify him." Phew! What a relief it was to hear that. I thought we weren't being told the whole story but, thankfully, clarification alleviated those fears. She took some information, explained the program, and went to her office to submit his application. She gave Austin a Make- A -Wish bracelet to wear, which he still has on today.

Another effort back home during these first days was a GoFundMe account set up on Austin's behalf by our friend Kelly. She has always been an event coordinator and knew how to organize an initiative such as this fundraiser. I felt rather awkward at first when she messaged me about it, but she knew what we were going to need even when we couldn't focus on that aspect of this situation. It was such a blessing to have her thinking of our welfare and taking the time to set up the account. By the second day, the fund had accrued enough to reach the goal set so Kelly increased it a bit higher to keep the momentum. David and I were just humbled at the love demonstrated through such giving and didn't know how to react. Other messages were coming in informing us of an account set up at a local bank by the show choir families, funds being donated by our employers, people wanting to send care packages, others wanting to pay for meals that we were buying in New Jersey and even an offer to fly Jamie up to be with us for a visit. How does one get their arms around such generosity? I just sobbed at the thought of everyone pouring out their prayers, gifts, and love from afar. They felt so far away yet in a strange sense felt like they were in the room. I could literally feel the spirit of people back home as well as friends and family around the country. I would say over and over to our Jersey team "Can you feel the Illinois people pulling him home, can you feel it?" They would laugh and agree that from the looks of the pictures, we had a great team working outside of the hospital too. God's work near and far....

We received an email from one of the organizations back home with which Austin was affiliated. They would purchase one plane ticket for us for any one of our relatives or friends to be able to fly out to New Jersey to visit Austin. Oh, wow! How would we decide who to bring to New Jersey? It just made sense to go with his grandma Connie, who we knew would want to come visit. My sister, Lori, already had a plan to come and would take care of her own arrangements. So, we presented Grandma Connie with the option and she was thrilled. We set her up with phone numbers and let them work out the details back home. What a wonderful way to help a family in need. She would be arriving in a couple days. We also heard from our friend Angie back home. She would be in New York City the next day with her daughter on a short, fun trip. She wanted to know if she could stop by and visit Austin and grab some things from out of my house to bring to me. Most important were my medication bottles, which I didn't think I would need as I packed for a six-day band trip. Clearly, I was going to need them now. So, the day was very busy with setting up plans and settling into the next steps for Austin. We were very anxious to get him to wake up, get off the ventilator, and assess what residual effects the surgery was going to leave him with for now. Prayers were pouring in for good outcomes.

CHAPTER 12

Music to Our Ears

April 24, 2018 Continued

Austin was taking his dear, sweet time waking up after they turned the sedation off. Part of the reason was that they had given him extra sedation to get through the MRI that morning. For brain images, it is imperative to have the patient lay as still as possible so they increased the drips to accommodate. During our wait, the music therapist, Melissa, stopped by again. She had introduced herself at admission but we really hadn't worked with her yet. She is full-time at the hospital and works with patients through music intervention. She plays the guitar, sings, and even offered to bring a keyboard to the bedside for Austin to play if he so desired later. We shared with her Austin's involvement in music back at school and all about the band trip. We told her that we had gone to the *Phantom of the Opera* and how Austin had looked forward to seeing the performance. She surprised us by bringing an iPad to the bedside with the *Phantom* soundtrack downloaded. She thought Austin would benefit by having it playing at his bedside. I decided not to wait until Austin was awake. I had her put it at the head of his bed and let the music flow into his ears, whether he was able to hear it or not. We did this often back in the days when I worked as a nurse in the critical care department. Music is powerful and can work wonders for healing. So, I was willing to try anything to get Austin to wake up.

I stepped out for lunch and David stayed by Austin's side. The security guards were starting to recognize us as we traveled about the hospital. To gain access to Pediatrics or PICU, you had to be cleared by them and a buzzer had to be activated to open the doors to the respective units. I was learning this routine rapidly. My sleeping room was right by their station so they sadly had to put up with me coming and going often. By now, we had taken over three different rooms in the unit—my sleeping room, a sleeping room for David, and Austin's room. They did not hesitate to make us comfortable. The social services person named Rose was working diligently on trying to find us a hotel close to the hospital, where we could stay for an affordable price. She was great to work with and made sure to sort through all our out-of-town needs with us. Gradually, our anxieties about being away from home were subsiding as staff at Barnabas looked out after us while many friends and family were taking care of our affairs back home. Every time I thought about a new concern, someone was eager to take ownership of resolving the issue. I even had my boyfriend, Simon, and friends Carrie and Darla looking after my elderly father back in Decatur, who had recently been released from the hospital. They stepped up without hesitation to stop by his apartment to check on him. Peace of mind!

When I got back from lunch, I walked into Austin's room and to my amazement, he was awake! I was dumbfounded! David shared that he had stood over him and begged him to PLEASE wake up. And then—he did. Between the *Phantom* music in one ear and his dad pleading in the other ear, it worked! Now, we could try to get that tube out of his throat. They needed the intensivist, respiratory therapist, and his nurse to be present for the extubation. Fortunately, we had Paige again for the day so I was hopeful that Austin would recognize her. My post describing the extubation:

We put the Phantom *soundtrack at the head of Austin's bed and with begging from his dad to wake up, he did it!! Once awake we were able to extubate (with* Phantom *theme song playing during the procedure, 2 doctors present, respiratory and 2 nurses) and let him breathe on his own. He started talking coherently within seconds asking for shower, pain medicine, what car am I in? Is that* Phantom*? Can I blow my nose? I'm doing cartwheels!*

I can't tell you how profound an experience this extubation was. It felt like a scene out of a movie to me, with the *Phantom* theme song resonating throughout the room, and such a great team all standing around as the tube was pulled. And then... music to our ears, even better than the *Phantom*, to hear our son's voice come out so clearly and so intentional. He knew what he wanted and was able to articulate his needs! I asked him to say my name and he said weakly, "Gail." I asked him to say his dad's name and out came, "David." Then, I went out on a limb and wanted to test his short-term memory—I had Paige ask him about who she was. Guess what...he mumbled, "Paige." My heart was racing and I couldn't stop my excitement. I was blown away by how much was happening right in front of me. Oh, how I prayed for this. Of course, it wasn't loud enough for Paige, so she made him say it again, but this time to say it loud. He belted out "Paige" in an annoyed sort of tone but we were thrilled and giddy and everyone in the room was ecstatic with his accomplishments. It is a moment I will remember for a lifetime. Prayers were being answered....

CHAPTER 13

He's Our Kid Too

April 25, 2018

found a picture on one of the band parent's postings of someone lighting a candle inside the St. Patrick's Cathedral in New York City. Many of the kids and chaperones stopped by the cathedral during one of the days in the city. I was told several kids lit candles for Austin. The picture made me cry like a baby. It was so poignant. I think the whole experience with Austin gave these kids a different perspective on life. I remember being in high school and thinking life would last forever. I had no concept of mortality. Your mind is full of things in the moment and thinking of the future is only occasional. I think having one of their own school peers going through such a critical illness made them stop and think about the meaning of life for just a moment in time, if not longer. To witness a classmate firsthand go through the symptoms leading up to hospitalization, and then hear from your leader that his brain will be operated on and he will be staying behind in New Jersey, has to elicit a myriad of thoughts in the group. I'm sure it was scary for some, unbelievable for others, and even unimaginable for a few. At fifteen, sixteen, or seventeen years old, they haven't had enough time in their young lives to put this experience in a conceptual framework in their minds. It may be a point in time that many will always remember and potentially reflect back upon in their lifetime as they develop a point of reference. Regardless, no matter the age or circumstances, it was definitely a hardship for us all.

This morning was very busy. My post:

> *Wow....what a robust morning. His oxygen, bladder catheter, head staples, nose drip pad are all discontinued. He's talking frequently and coherently. Yes!! He drank water and moves all extremities. Left side is weaker than right. Both eyes are swollen shut but he insists on holding the water and doing it himself (just like him!). The neurosurgery team took his case and MRI and CT scans before the New Jersey and New York consortium of neurosurgeons yesterday and made a collective decision on how to move forward with his care. I was speechless and moved to tears when they shared this that they would give our kid all this attention. Their response – "he's our kid too." Mind-blowing. Then the infectious disease doctor came in and talked to us for an hour about the case and the bacteria specifics and basic anatomy and physiology and I swear it was like listening to a Harvard microbiology professor in the best layman's terms I've ever experienced. 1 whole hour..... they are putting his application into Make- A- Wish because he has a life- threatening illness but not terminal. He is blessed with this village and even more so by the village you all have created back home and around the country with our family and remote FB friends. Thank you for the GoFundMe donations, we are humbled by that as well as your magnitude of prayers, gifts, help with Jamie, dogs, household help, airfare, private plane offers and planned visits. So blessed.....so appreciative......so*

*amazed by the energy and spirit WE all have cre-
ated. THANK YOU!!!*

I was having trouble understanding exactly what type of consortium this neurosurgery group was but many residents attend it and I think one of our lead physician's residents did the presentation. They said the room was full and about forty neurosurgeons were in attendance. We were told many times since Austin was admitted how rare his problem was and, sadly, they had seen four kids with the same problem come in this past month. There was grave concern verbalized by many of our physicians on our team that they didn't know why they were seeing an increase in incidence of this sinus complication. I asked the ENT group if there was anything that I could have done differently to have avoided this whole situation. They told me no; we had just been unlucky. They said that maybe a different antibiotic prescribed with Austin's first sinus infection back in March would have helped to prevent the abscess but more research is needed and they would be publishing recommendations down the road in collaboration with neurosurgery. I asked when that would be available to read and gingerly they reminded me that the publication process doesn't happen overnight. Yes, I knew this to be true. They said that Austin's case would definitely be part of the study group.

As word got out to our friends and family that I was hanging pictures on the wall in Austin's room, I started getting flooded with pictures emailed and texted up to me. I'm not sure how deep everyone had to go to find some of those treasures but wow, were they classics from the past. I get emotional on a normal day just looking at pictures from when the boys were little. Can you imagine how it was to look at these pictures on that day? I once took care of a young lady who had been in a tornado and had lost one of her legs during the event. Her mother told me that she was never able to look at photos of her daughter from the childhood years the same anymore. I've never forgotten that statement and often wondered what it would be like for that mother. Her daughter had thankfully survived an egregious storm but yet life would never be the same with an amputated leg. And how does one ever psychologically get over thoughts of being in that storm, especially when dangerous weather patterns continue to evolve at any given time? I remember the patient struggling emotionally with the loss of her leg. Clearly, her mother (who loved her daughter unconditionally) was grieving with a sense of loss too—her vision of that child fully intact and living a basically normal life. I had those fleeting moments too and I'm wondering if maybe this is part of normal coping. However, thoughts like that are very benign and lead you to think about how much you love your son no matter what his circumstances are. So, I loved the pictures and had as many of them laminated as possible without wearing out my welcome with the child life coordinator. She was so gracious when I asked her to print them all out and laminate as well. It really brought Austin's personality into the room and let the staff come to know the kid in front of them. We were asked so many questions about his life when they perused the photos. One person even said, "This Mt. Zion town sure shows a unique sense of community; how cool they seem." Of course, I agreed. Even friends who had moved away from Mt. Zion sent in pictures. I could hardly wait for Austin to be able to open his eyes and see them. We were just waiting for the swelling to go down. Until that happened, we were left with only being able to describe this mural to him and read out loud any communications that were coming in via Facebook, texts, and emails. His exact words: "It's insane out there!" It was a great compliment spoken from a teenager perspective.

CHAPTER 14

Grandma Arrives

April 26, 2018

I received an early text this morning from my friend Carrie back home. Her son PJ is good friends with Austin and was going crazy because he saw activity on his Snap Maps site that led him to believe Austin had been on the application. I told Carrie it was not possible since Austin's eyes were completely swollen shut and he was not able to use his cell phone yet. She said the kids in Austin's friends circle insisted that they were right and then she proceeded to send me a screenshot of a picture showing what they call Austin's bitmoji. Yep, there he was (you would have to understand Snap Maps to know what this all means), standing in New Jersey at St. Barnabas Medical Center. I was astounded. I thought over and over how this was possible. Then I remembered Austin asking to have his phone the day before and wondering why he wanted it. I hadn't paid attention after I gave it to him but he obviously wanted to get on his Snap Chat and do what's called *save your streaks*. I had to laugh out loud as I thought about what he was trying to do. Then I thought, "Well, he may possibly be the first blind person to have been on Snap Maps." Yes, my friend Carrie, your son was right....

Austin's Bitmoji

I got another text that morning from my friend Angie stating that she would be by that morning to see Austin and to drop off things from my house, as well as other items from friends back home. She would be taking an Uber service from NYC over to the hospital. I just was so surprised that someone would consider taking time out from her trip to do this for us. It touched my heart. She arrived an hour later. It felt so comforting having someone from home finally to sit and chat with. I didn't realize how homesick I really was until we started talking. We sat in the lobby of Barnabas for about a half hour debriefing on all that had happened. I couldn't keep myself from crying, ultimately. After all, she was the first person from home in front of me to hear our saga and to literally see the fatigue and stress we were under. I think I looked like death warmed over. Angie didn't care how I looked, though. She was there to love and support us and when I took her to the bedside to see Austin, she even gathered us in a circle over Austin and led a prayer for healing. I am in awe of how she just knew the right things to say and left us with such a sense of peace in our hearts. I love this girl. She leads her life like this every day—faith-based, genuine, caring, and giving. She radiates with spirit when you're around her and I'll never forget how she reached out to us this day. The kids back at Mt. Zion high school had passed a *Get Well Soon* sign around and wrote inspirational messages on it for Austin to have. Angie draped this sign on Austin before we prayed. It almost seemed like a prayer quilt in that moment. We ended up hanging it on the wall by the pictures so that he could look at it later when his eyes were open. She also gave us a bag of cards from our Mt. Zion teachers and friends. People were just so generous with their donations. It meant a lot for her to bring those to us. I walked her out to her Uber ride and hugged her goodbye. I was so grateful for the visit. It definitely lifted my spirits and we all appreciated it.

Angie with Mt. Zion Well Wishes Poster

David had to leave shortly after Angie to go pick his mother, Connie, up from the Newark airport. She had flown in from Decatur and would be staying for five days. We had worked closely with social services to secure a hotel before her arrival.

There weren't very many to choose from without a long drive. We settled on one that we thought would work. Sadly, it turned out to be quite a disappointment and they canceled the reservation on the spot. Anxious to see Austin, they grabbed lunch and headed to the hospital. Austin was very excited to have his grandma there. They chatted for a bit but Austin still drifted in and out of sleep during the early days after surgery so she sat by his side as he slept and visited with us. There was a lot to catch her up on. I headed out to look for other hotels hoping to see the inside of the hotel this time instead of making online or phone reservations. We were very unfamiliar with the area so it was good to explore lodging firsthand. Ultimately, we landed in a reputable chain hotel in West Orange, NJ, which was fifteen minutes from the hospital. They gave us a small discount for medical purposes but were still fairly expensive compared to Illinois prices. I would soon learn that the cost of living where we were in New Jersey was significantly higher than that of Central Illinois. This was even more of an incentive to hurry up and get back home. The funds left by the band kids and chaperones were invaluable as we learned about expenses the hard way. Even gas was at premium prices not only due to geography but also because New Jersey is a full-service mandate at the pumps. I needed gas as I left to head back to the hospital. After turning off the car and releasing the gas tank cap I stepped out to grab the nozzle and was taken aback as a man approached my van. I thought he was going to start trouble with me but then he grabbed the nozzle before me and started to put it into the tank. I barked "What are you doing?" He looked surprised and responded in a sheepish voice, "Um, giving you full service?" I never laughed so hard. Here I thought I was getting accosted and the poor guy was just doing his job. I did not realize that New Jersey was the only state with this law. I actually rather enjoyed not having to do the work but did not enjoy the price of gas. I asked if I could take his picture and show my friends because I thought it was so funny. He replied, "Sure! I've worked here for four years and never had anyone ask to take my picture." It gave me a great conversation piece for a week. Isn't it fun to tell stories against yourself for the entertainment of others? If you can't laugh at yourself once in a while then you need to do some introspection to see why not. I think admitting your "brain vacations" shows that we are all human and make silly mistakes. Yes, that was quite entertaining to the Jersey people back at Barnabas.

When I got back to the bedside I couldn't believe the miracles I was witnessing. Just in the two hours that I was away, some swelling had gone down (we were pumping steroids into him hoping for this) and Austin was now sitting there with open eyes! Hooray! Also, his left hand had started moving. I was so scared that this was going to take weeks to get back and here he was moving it within days of surgery. David had dressed him in a regular shirt and shorts and did away with the hospital gown. He looked so much more like himself. We were getting there inch by inch. I was sure Angie's prayers had helped and were being answered. I was thrilled that Grandma was there to see this, too. Everything came together and he was making progress in the right direction. And the prayers from home were going viral. We had several churches back home add him to prayer lists and chains. Families were praying together for him. I was receiving loads of prayers through my Facebook site. I continued telling the staff, "Can you feel Illinois praying for him? Can you feel them pulling him back home? They're banding together." I could not stop thanking God for all He was doing. Austin was making his way back....

CHAPTER 15

#FykeItUp is Born

April 27, 2018

C ell phones can be your friend or foe. When they are used as a makeshift call light to summon the attention of a parent, I was not so sure I was too thrilled about Austin having full use of it again. But he was in a scary place and going through the worst experience of his life, so I was happy that he reached out to me even if it meant interrupted sleep. My post that morning:

> *Well, last night was rough. Austin can use his phone now so the texts were off and on every 2 hours throughout the night complaining about various things. At 6a I finally left my sleeping room and came to the bedside to find him in a panic attack mode. It turned out to be lack of pain control and once the morphine was increased, he is fine. Neurosurgery team took all his staples out today from his head and discontinued the "brain drain" or JP drain as we say in healthcare terms. He is craving a Subway sandwich which is first food request in 8 days. That will make the band director happy to know he will eat finally. We begged him to eat on the band trip and he refused.*

Today he will walk in the halls, hopefully get IV off and be able to take more pills instead of IV meds. They said his move to Chicago will be a private jet because it is too far for a helicopter. Not sure when that will be. We still have another surgery on Tuesday to rinse the sinuses again and then we will convene as a team with all his doctors together at one table to create the discharge plan.

Austin's grandma Connie flew in safely yesterday and is here until Monday and then my sister arrives next Thursday. My brother Gary is driving down to be with Jamie next week for a few days to give Jennifer a break plus give Jamie time back at his house. My friends Charlotte and Ken have a friend nearby me that is willing to do laundry for us. I'm calling her today. At a point of exhaustion where I am thrilled to bring her on board. We have been receiving cards of love, support and donations and GoFundMe donations and other bank deposits to help with this journey and cannot express enough gratitude. So so humbled. The Taylorville band program donated to Austin in the GoFundMe account as well and Austin doesn't know why because he doesn't know them but I think these are lessons to him in giving and why we do what we do. So, out of every hardship there are good things that can evolve and your acts of faith, generosity, love, and inspiration will prevail within that realm. With that Austin cannot fail....#FykeItUp

The previous night, I had been texting with Austin's band friends Jacob and Matt and insisted that they create a hashtag for this whole crazy experience. They were in the middle of Combo practice coming up with silly ideas, which gave Austin a lot of laughs. He thinks the world of those two and was really missing them. After much joking, they settled on **#FykeItUp**, which I started using immediately to close my posts. They would be in charge of getting it going back in Mt. Zion and we would create the stir at Barnabas and with others back home. It was rather fun. We made a sign with the hashtag on it and had staff take turns holding it for a picture. Then we left the sign posted on the wall by all the other pictures. With Austin's eyes being open now he was able to read the cards from the band kids, see the poster on the wall with all the messages from back home, and look at the other cards that had arrived. He said it made his day to see all these things that people had been doing. Kathi, the person who had offered to do our laundry, came today. We visited in the lobby for a while and really connected on all levels. She told me about her friendship with Ken (a nurse that works with me back home at my hospital) from childhood days. It's always fun to reflect on all the stories that we've banked in our minds over the years. I enjoyed listening to her and was impressed that they had stayed in touch all those years. Ken and his wife, Charlotte, thought Kathi would be a good person to help me because she had Illinois roots and still had that southern Illinois hospitality about her. They were right. I gave her the laundry and she promised to be back in a couple days with it. Getting to a laundromat right now was not an option with all the activities going on with Austin. I let down the fierce shield I usually hold up when someone offers to help and let her help. I felt a great sense of relief from having her there. Although we're not a generation apart, she felt like a mother to me at the moment.

Our hashtag for this experience

Child Life Coordinator Laura joining in on the fun

My "new" New Jersey friend Kathi

The day went well for Austin. He was able to walk in the hall with help today and tolerated it very well. They talked about moving up his discharge date because he was exceeding therapy goals. This was such great news for all. The physicians disclosed that the bone will not be usable for the skull rebuild because of the infection risk so a synthetic structure would be created for the rebuild. They did not tell us exactly what the structure would be made of but I thought someone mentioned titanium. We would ask those questions later. I touched base with Jamie via FaceTime on our phones at the dinner hour. It was good to see his face. We missed him so much but he was doing well and seemed happy. Just for fun, I walked around St. Barnabas and showed him all the different areas on FaceTime. We had been telling him about the hospital but it was a lot of fun to walk outside and show him the building all lit up in neon green lights and show him the cafeteria we had been using and our sleeping rooms. I ended the tour in Austin's room and showed him all around there too. We opted not to show him

Austin yet as we didn't want him to be sad to see his brother so swollen.

The last bit of news for the night was videos and pictures being sent to us from the Mt. Zion High School Spring Show. Austin was to have been playing his saxophone for the performances that weekend but fortunately, his friend Jacob stepped up and covered his spot for him and did a great job from what I heard. The assistant director of the show choirs, Heather, put a shout out on stage to Austin and announced that they would be having collection buckets in the foyer for anyone wanting to help with medical expenses. We were so thankful for the efforts and appreciated everyone recording the announcement for us. Modern technology was key in our whole stay at Barnabas. There were so many times when people sent us recordings or pictures of things they were doing on Austin's behalf back home. Our family felt loved, and people were easing the pain of this whole ordeal. Everyone back home carried us through the days, even hours, and provided energy in the room that was so desperately needed.

CHAPTER 16

If Only He Would Eat

April 28, 2018

After seven days of being at the hospital almost nonstop and not sleeping much between days, I was really getting stir-crazy. Many years ago, when I worked in critical care nursing we called it ICU psychosis. If you think about it, patients and family members are cooped up in a small space sitting in basically the same chair off and on (or, as a patient, mostly in bed), listening to a variety of bells and whistles. There's not much diversion except for a television, your phone, and staff coming in and out of the room. We made conversation often and tried to keep Austin's spirits up. Having Grandma there was wonderful as she was very calming for Austin and also chimed into the conversations. Telling stories from Austin's younger years even provided some laughter. But beyond this, I completely understand why families become restless, bored, irritated, and stressed out. If I could reinvent hospital and doctor office space, I would add diversional activities for patients and families. Whatever it might be would not cause infection control issues, would be safe for children to be around, would not break within two days, and would not be something that people would be tempted to steal. Ha! Can you tell there have been issues over the years with installing items in a patient room? I'm sure hotels struggle with the same barriers. But for now, we were all getting tired of being in the hospital, especially Austin. My post that day:

Patients get ICU psychosis and family members do as well. We are all 3 at that point so I recognized the need to get out of the building and just go somewhere, anywhere. I decided to do my journey without a compass or GPS on the phone and just drive forward. I wanted to see where God would take me. After all we haven't had a compass all week of I really haven't had any clue on where I've been for the past 9 days. I let the bus just take me to NYC with a few checks on my phone as I was tired of riding. The bus navigated for me until Sunday morning and then was absolutely no clue in my head where I was between hospitals and such. Even on Sat when the group was gone I had to walk a mile to get to the closest restaurant or opt for items out of the hotel gift shop to eat. I just walked until I found Fuddrucker's up the road. So no compass today, who needs it when you have no compass at the bedside of your child either. You follow God's lead you use common sense and you take risks at times. I stumbled first into West Orange and found a cool bakery and ate on a park bench on a beautiful sunny 65 degree day. No one bothered me and it was great meditation. Then the van took me to Orange which looks a little rough but I am opting out of getting out of the van but instead found this cool church with beautiful architecture. I'm in their parking lot praying for Austin today and finishing my devotions for the day. It seems like a safe haven in the middle of a tough neighborhood.

The bakery kid that rang me up asked why I was here in NJ when he heard I was from Illinois. He's now on the prayer chain too. Austin is having a challenging time eating. He wants nothing and hasn't eaten in 10 days now. A feeding tube lingers in the room threatening to be his near future in order to get nutrition for brain healing. We have thrown pizza and Subway and crackers and shakes and drinks and all of his requests at him only for him to stare at it and push it away. This is my kid that eats me out of house and home on a normal day. It will certainly delay his discharge if we cannot get over this hump. Other than that he is to get a shower for the first time as I am out and about which should make him happy. We are still changing the pain meds around to try to find a way to eliminate the psychosis pattern. He has his days and nights mixed up too which just contributes to the overall stress of the situation. But I have taken care of many before him with this exact behavior pattern and ultimately we land on our feet. It just takes patience and trials and teamwork.

#FykeItUp

With everything going on with Austin, the last problem I expected was to have his appetite gone after surgery. I thought surely with the infection cleaned out that he would regain his food cravings and put the weight back on that he had lost. At this point, he was down twenty pounds. The dietician on rounds had suggested that we bring in favorite foods but even that had failed. They were sending up Ensure drinks and puddings but nothing would work. For a moment, I was afraid that the surgery had permanently altered either his sense of smell or his sense of taste. I didn't want to think about permanent problems. We were making such good progress. We would keep trying and maybe the tide would turn....

CHAPTER 17

A Day of Many Blessings

April 29, 2018

would have to declare this day as the most diverse day that we had in New Jersey. I had several friends suggest that I go back and tell Breakfast Lady at the hotel in Parsippany that she had saved Austin's life. I found that to be a great idea and decided to go back and thank her, as well as drop off a gift. Her name was actually Karla and I will be indebted to her for life. She saved my son's life. What better gift can a mother ask for? More so, what gift could I give her that was representative of the gratitude that Austin's family and friends felt? I decided that no matter what I did it would never be enough so a visit would have to do. I had called the hotel ahead of time to make sure that she would be working the breakfast area that day and fortunately she was on duty. When I walked into the dining area, there she was, bustling around as expected. I approached her and a broad grin came over her face as if she knew exactly who I was. Yes, she indeed knew who I was and told me that she had heard about Austin from the other staff. I told her that he was doing well and showed her some pictures from the hospital. Then I gave her a hug and thanked her for saving him and that I was forever going to remember her. She graciously accepted my thanks and the card I gave her and told me she loved us and apologized for having to keep moving to take care of her customers. I promised to bring Austin by to visit her sometime next year when he was all healed and back to his old self. That made her smile and, just like that, she was back to work. I glanced back at her one last time as I headed to the door and thought for a moment on what would have happened if I had turned a deaf ear to her. I've asked myself that same question probably a hundred times since that day.

Me with Breakfast Lady

When I got back to the hotel, I met Kathi in the lobby again to take back my clean laundry from her. She also had put several other items in the bag to make it like a care package. One of the items was a St. Barnabas t-shirt which she had left over from an event that she had coordinated at one time on campus there. I wore it many times after that day and some people actually thought I worked there when I was wearing it. She stayed again for a half hour or so just to visit and I updated her on all the progress Austin had made over the weekend. She promised she would think about a trip back to Illinois sometime soon to see her friends and would let me know if she was in the area. I was inspired by her kindness that she provided to total strangers and thought about how I would pay that forward someday to others.

I headed up to Austin's room from there—doing the usual parking ticket payment of the day and clearing through the security posts. I had the processes down now! When I entered the room, I was amazed at how good Austin looked. My post that day:

> *Your prayers have continued to move us forward. I posted yesterday the need to get out and about due to ICU psychosis. When I came back I had a new kid. His demeanor was completely changed back to his old self. He was eating a little more and had showered and was just feeling so much better. Every time I leave and come back this seems to happen so maybe I better leave more often, LOL. He slept all night and did not text me at all. This morning his nurse brought us in New Jersey bagels and we both had the best bagel ever. He chased it with a chocolate milk and seems to be getting over the food problem. We got news today that the inpatient stay in Chicago should be very brief because he is doing better than expected. His left hand is really coming alive. The neurosurgeons told me that the skull rebuild will not be difficult so I am very, very excited by all of this news!!! Thank you prayer chains and lists and warriors!!!*
>
> *#FykeItUp*

The next excursion to the lobby was to meet up with a gentleman named Joe from Hannah's Care Packages. My friend Sandy signed us up for this program since she had learned about them when her son was hospitalized in St. Louis. It is a nationwide program and she thought we would appreciate their services since we were so far from home and getting by only on the bare minimum of personal supplies. She knew that we were going through a fearful situation as well, which is another reason that Hannah's Care Packages was created— to help families cope. According to what I was told, Hannah's Care Packages helps families of children with life-threatening illnesses by bringing a care package full of toiletries, journals, pens, hair ties, combs and brushes, snacks, and more along with a warm smile and friendly conversation. They help to encourage and bring hope to the moms and dads of the children who are such brave warriors as they are going through their struggles with illness. Joe was a volunteer for the program and shared that he goes all over New Jersey with his visits. He is a full-time pharmacist and volunteers for Hannah's in his free time. He was a very nice guy and we were excited to have him stop by to see Austin. He stayed at the bedside for about fifteen to twenty minutes and then had to head out for the day. I was in awe that Sandy and her family went through a hardship with her son and was now in a place where she could pay it forward to the next family. We have to do this for each other. To love one another in such a way is truly impactful and something that is remembered forever. We probably would not have known about this program if not for Sandy. St. Barnabas had many support services for pediatric patients but I'm not sure that they were aware of Hannah's Care Packages.

Joe, myself, Connie, and David

My phone started lighting up with messages from back home in the afternoon related to a special dedication to Austin from the show choir kids. They had finished up for the weekend with the Spring Show and Senior Spotlights and then proceeded to do a balloon release in the parking lot of the Mt Zion high school. All the balloons had Austin's hashtag **#FykeItUp** on them and one of the adults shouted, "1,2,3" and off the balloons drifted with the crowd shouts of, "FykeItUp." I played it for Austin and he was deeply touched. I sent a text to one of the show choir parents asking who had coordinated the event and done all the work on the balloons and she responded that it was a team effort and everyone helped. It was another way that we felt so connected over the miles. Of course, I had to show it to the nurses. They loved it.

The final trip of the day to the lobby was to greet the family of my friends Al and Lesley. I went to high school with them back in the 1980s and have been friends with them ever since. Lesley was following our journey on Facebook. Al's sister lives in Parsippany and was willing to help us out in any way. Lesley had informed her of Austin's illness. I was given her phone number and I called her. She offered to bring a meal to us, which I immediately accepted because, by now, hospital food and takeout food were getting old. The thought of a home-cooked meal was divine. Her name was Sandy and her daughter, Jennifer, also wanted to help. The two of them brought us enough food to feed an army. I was overwhelmed by their generosity. They had even stopped at a Target store before coming to the hospital and picked up a couple of items that we needed. When I asked to reimburse them for the items they refused and just wanted to call it a donation. Total strangers to us—who just wanted to help people in need. There is so much good in the world. I intend to look for it under normal conditions. I think we all should. Why wait for a catastrophic illness to care for each other? What would it look like if we just did things like this for each other for no reason? I gave them hugs after they brought all the food in and took it up to the room. There was literally enough to feed our family and the whole night shift of the PICU department. We set up a buffet at the nurse's station and shared with everyone. As I have witnessed over the past thirty-one years, food always works well for healthcare staff. They were grateful for the feast. It was a busy day indeed, but a day full of many blessings!

CHAPTER 18

Pet Therapy Is Better than Any Medication

April 30, 2018

This morning, Austin and I were having a discussion about hospital-induced depression and being homesick. We had been in Barnabas for nine days now and he was tired of the same four walls. One of the nurses, Laura, had taken him outside yesterday for a ride in the wheelchair and that was very helpful. We just looped around the front of the hospital and then back in through a side door but it was great for him to get fresh air. The wind was still a bit brisk and the temperature was still in the fifties but at least it was warmer than the day that we had been out at the Statue of Liberty waiting in line with a temperature of forty-five degrees accompanied by a fierce wind. I was starting to see the buds on the trees and knew that spring was right around the corner. I was hoping that we wouldn't still be here in New Jersey at the change in seasons. Yes, I guess we were all a bit homesick. Right in the middle of our discussion, a dog named Cody came into the room with his owner. Cody is one of the pet therapists at St. Barnabas. We were told that there were fifty-six pet therapists on staff and that the owners of the dogs scheduled visiting rounds through coordinating efforts of the volunteer department. The dogs and their owners get eight weeks of training (two hours a week) to qualify for this role. At the end of the course, the dog and owner must take an exam with a passing score before being allowed to be a pet therapist. Austin absolutely loved the dogs. His sadness would immediately leave when the dogs entered the room. When the dogs left, Austin would be in a great mood the rest of the day. I had never seen such an impacting intervention as this pet therapy. So many people turn toward medications or less optimal solutions when faced with adversity. Why not consider the unconditional love of a dog? The beauty of having an organization offering the visits with a pet is that the recipient need not be the owner. Some people may not desire to take care of an animal or have the appropriate living arrangement for one but the option of having intermittent visits organized by others may possibly serve the need. David and I were joking that they probably had a dog outside the curtain just waiting for the moments when they sensed Austin needed them. Their timing was perfect. Our perception was that a dog walked in every time Austin was having a low moment.

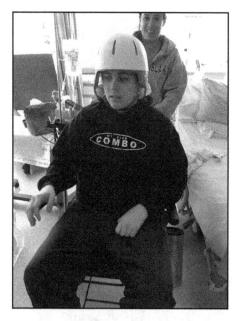

Austin and Laura

Austin was also sad that day because his grandma had to fly back to Illinois. It had been comforting having her there and she had spent a lot of time calming Austin and reassuring him that he was doing well. She had been there when he was first able to get out of bed with the helmet on and had been there to see much of his progress. We said our goodbyes and then David took her back to the Newark airport for departure. Hopefully, the next time she saw Austin he would look even more like himself—and feel like himself. His world was still a bit upside down and we had a long road ahead of us. That afternoon, he had another MRI under general anesthesia in preparation for his next sinus lavage to be performed by the ENT team. It was basically a progress check on the sinuses to make sure all the infection was still clear from the original surgery. We had been told up front that he would have a series of two to three sinus cleansings before this was all over and done with. Fortunately, they told us that the last cleansing could be done by an ENT back home in Decatur, Illinois.

The rest of the day was uneventful and this was just fine with us. Quiet times were nice and Austin still required nap periods. We would turn off the lights and sit peacefully in a darkened room with the television set on low volume. Nurses would sneak in to do their vital signs checks and medications but they were always respectful of Austin's nap times. From a nursing perspective, this usually requires intentional efforts as we are wide awake and bustling about all day and our energy levels sometimes accompany us into the rooms. In my mind, it is equivalent to Wall Street guys leaving the trading floor and stepping into a library—ask any nurse (I'm smiling as I wrote that last sentence). Here is my post from that night:

> *It was hard to drive away from the hospital tonight and stay in a hotel after 12 days of this night-mare. I've been on a futon in a tiny sleeping room in order to be close by for problems or if Austin needed me. His dad is staying in a sleeping room tonight. It hopefully will be quiet. So this hotel*

is like a vacation with a real bed and the convenience of an attached bathroom and shower!

Austin and his Dad and I have been on a similar nightmare together at the time of his birth. He was a premature baby and I was so sick with preeclampsia. He aspirated fluids during the birthing process and then got a respiratory viral infection two days into life. We about lost him. Austin and I both spent two weeks in the hospital. So we fought together then and we'll fight this one too. I remember feeling hopeless at the thought of losing him almost 16 years ago......kind of similar to the feeling I had last Sunday in the St. Clare's ER. It's like you're smacked across the face and stunned until reality commands you to wake up and make split second decisions and make the right decisions because the stakes are high. The world is on your shoulders. Don't crumble! So, I feel as if all the big decisions have been made moving forward, decisions on how to be the best mom possible for the next few months. Part of that includes having the courage to let people help and let others do things to carry your burdens and walk away knowing you have done all that you have the power to do.

So for tonight, I'm only a 20 minute drive away and his dad is there. He's in good hands at an excellent hospital. I'm putting my faith in God that he is fine and I'm finally going to sleep.

#FykeItUp

CHAPTER 19

Austin Meets Austin

May 1, 2018

The morning started with some challenging news. The lead neurosurgeon made rounds and said there was still a tiny bit of abscess left in the frontal region of Austin's brain, which he wanted to follow just a bit longer but was thinking it would be taken care of by antibiotics. He said he wanted to look at it by MRI on Saturday (four days from then) and make the discharge plan at that time. Austin took the news tearfully but then prayers kept working and randomly another therapy dog showed up on rounds. He jumped up on the foot of Austin's bed and smiles were immediately induced from Austin. I couldn't believe the timing of the visit and all by chance. Then, I looked at his name tag and about fell over—really? His name was Austin as well! Who names a dog Austin?? I'd never heard of it before but here he was, cheering our Austin up. It was at that moment that I felt the need to get more versed in pet therapy once I returned home. Even before the trip to NYC, I had been hearing about pet therapy within the prison systems. I thought it was a great idea for those individuals who have never been shown love in their lifetime and would benefit from the unconditional love of an animal. I had people respond to my posts that there was a local organization in Decatur, Illinois that offered pet therapy called PawPrints Ministries. I intended to get in touch with the owner at first avail.

Austin with Pet therapist Austin

Austin eventually went down to surgery for his second sinus lavage. He wasn't gone very long and tolerated the surgery well. He experienced some pain that evening but took pain meds to keep comfortable. The good news was that there was no sign of any infection when they were doing the procedure. We were so relieved and thankful for yet more prayers answered. These sinuses had been the original culprit that invaded the brain tissue with infectious exudate and I still hadn't forgiven them for wreaking havoc. I stayed at the hospital for as long as I could in the evenings but the events of the days always wore me out and I tended to lose my stamina by 8 p.m. or 9 p.m. routinely. David has always had the ability to hold out longer and generally stayed with Austin until he was ready to go to sleep for the night. He had been very attentive to all of Austin's needs throughout the hospitalization and the staff gave him many compliments on how well he took care of Austin. He had stayed home when Austin was a baby and cared for him, as well as his brother Jamie when he was born, so he knew how to anticipate what Austin needed even before he would ask for things. I had the experience of pushing IV pumps around and managing heart monitor equipment from years of nursing but I let David help Austin with all the cords without being bossy on how to do it and tried to let him ask his own questions of the physicians or nurses as he worried about different things. His questions were excellent and sometimes things that I hadn't thought of. So, we made a good team as we tried to support Austin to the best of our ability. I laid down that night thinking about what the next days would bring and remembered that my sister would be flying in soon. I was so excited that she was coming. Austin loves his Aunt Lori.

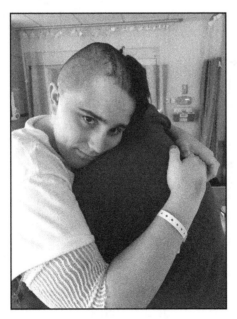

Austin with David

CHAPTER 20

Tim Comes to Visit

May 2, 2018

Before I could even leave the hotel that morning I was getting texts from Austin to bring him food! Music to my ears!! I would have gone anywhere to bring him food today. I brought him spaghetti because that is what sounded good to him at the moment. I had discovered a restaurant with soft pretzel themed selections the other day while out on a Target run and so for lunch, he wanted food from there. Off I went! We were on a roll. I was so afraid that he would get all this food in his system and then get deathly ill from overeating. Not the case—the requests kept coming in. We were charged with finding him a steak for dinner. That was going to be tough because I had no idea where to find steak. David spent an hour searching the Internet. The staff didn't really have any ideas for us. We finally discovered a place about ten minutes away, so we called in a takeout order to them later. We then got a surprise text from our friend Tim who was Austin's friend in faith (his adult mentor) from the church back home. He was in the area vacationing at his sister's house on Staten Island and wanted to drop by for a visit. Of course! What a welcome surprise! First Angie, now Tim. We felt very blessed that people would go to such measures. He would be there later in the day.

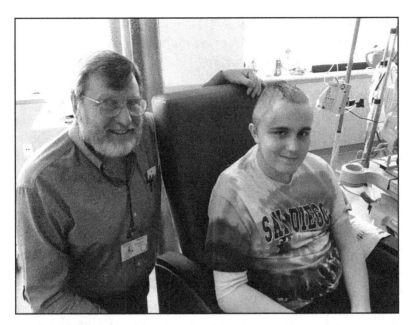

Austin and Tim

The big debate of the day was how to get Austin to Chicago. Could the brain handle the pressurized cabin? Would he qualify for a critical care transport mode with insurance? If not, could we take ground transportation? Case management would be starting to work out these details but we had to get input from the physicians before proceeding. We were scheduled for a team meeting the next day at 7 a.m. to start a discussion about the discharge plan details. We had so many questions about transport, driver's license, playing the saxophone, and getting set up in Chicago. There were many burning questions that Austin needed to be answered in order to be less in a quandary and more realistic with his expectations. We had gone round and round on what marching band season would look like for him in the fall. Mr. Ward had sent multiple messages to us that he would work closely with Austin's restrictions and keep him as involved as possible in the upcoming marching season. The other conversation that frequented the room was when a driver's license would be possible. Austin had been on an antiepileptic medication since admission just for precautionary purposes and there was concern that the state of Illinois would not let him drive with this medication on board. He wouldn't have to take it for the rest of his life but no one was really able to tell us how long he would be on the medication. I think they wanted the team in Chicago to make that decision, so we would have to wait for answers about driving.

The music therapist at the hospital, Melissa, had been patiently trying to spend time with Austin since day one but always lost out due to timing. She had offered to play her guitar during his PICC (peripherally inserted central catheter) line insertion but he declined because he just wasn't feeling well at the time. She had brought the iPad with *Phantom* music and had also brought him a keyboard to play at his leisure. Today, Austin asked for the keyboard and was able to play some songs by ear. I noticed that the keyboard served a dual purpose as it also provided strength training for his left hand while playing. We appreciated Melissa's patience as anyone else probably would have given up trying to work with Austin. She understood what he was going through and was probably familiar with having to work around the distractions of a hospital. I just kept hoping as she left each day that she would return some time and it would be perfect timing. I would get my wishes answered later. Meanwhile, Tim came by and we were so happy to see him. Austin enjoyed his visits and found him to be very funny. Tim brought cookies from a Staten Island bakery that we all enjoyed. He also brought gifts for Austin from his recent travels. While he was there, the humor team stopped in to entertain Austin. We had seen these guys a few days earlier but were too busy to have them stop. At the time, I was happy that we were busy because they were dressed as clowns and Austin doesn't like clowns. But today, they just came right in and started in on their act. They really didn't give me time to tell them "no thank you," and Tim was welcoming to them so I just let it happen. Before long, I found myself just laughing and laughing and Austin was as well. Then they alluded to Austin being a musician so they scored points in my mind and suddenly I thought maybe I liked them. But it wasn't until one of them pulled out a fairly good-sized syringe and started playing it like a woodwind instrument. It sounded awesome! I was truly impressed. The song was familiar but I didn't know the name of it. Tim, on the other hand, knew the words to the song and started singing. We were now rolling with laughter. The song was called "The Girl from Ipanema." I made sure that I sent a text to Mr. Ward that there was a new woodwind instrument out there that he should consider adding to the band room. Ha!

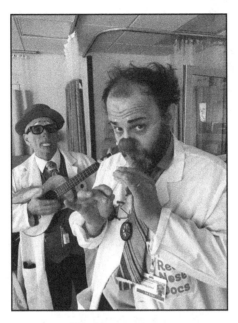

The Humor team

After the humor team left, Tim and I decided to connect with our pastor back in Decatur and get him on speaker phone. Pastor Mike answered right away and was happy to hear that Tim had stopped by. He informed us that he had networked with the pastor in Livingston, New Jersey, from the Methodist church and that he would be able to stop by to visit. Pastor Mike had also been working all week to find us connections for hotel rooms. Then, there was our youth leader, Kyle, who had coordinated getting a care package to us with snacks, gift cards, a prayer shawl, and other items for Austin. I do have to mention that Kyle included a basketball hoop to hang up in the hospital room but Austin thought he would knock medications out of a nurse's hands and get in trouble. Or he thought he might hit a physician on rounds with a basketball, so he opted out of hanging up the hoop. But it sure was tempting! The church was also raising funds from the congregation to donate toward our medical expenses. I've been at the First United Methodist in Decatur for fifty-three years (I may have the title as longest membership or at least, second only to Bill Brown) and the efforts shown toward our family were the same I have seen for many others over the years. If you need help, we're there with our prayers, gifts, and love. Yes, they were there with their prayers, gifts, and love. And we loved them for it.

The last thing Tim did before leaving for the day was to accompany me to the restaurant to get Austin steak for his dinner. On the drive, we decided to cruise past the Methodist church just to see what it looked like and to get some pictures to send back to Pastor Mike. We looked silly, running across their lawn to get close-up pictures but we decided to claim we were Illinois tourists if anyone questioned us. Austin thoroughly enjoyed the steak and baked potato that we brought him and it was at this point that we decided the poor appetite era may have ended. Hallelujah! No feeding tubes! More prayers answered....

Back at the hotel that night, I was reflecting on the day and feeling hopeful. We had made Austin laugh today, enjoyed the not-so-creepy clowns, had three successful meals, and received word that a local pastor was joining our Jersey team of caregivers. Yes, we were on a good path and for this, I was praising God. He had surrounded us with so much good that it was hard to dwell on the bad or feel sorry for ourselves. I was starting to think about how the days were going in general as well. I was beginning to understand the Jersey way of life. Here was my post before bedtime:

> *After being at St. Barnabas for 12 days I have noticed that we have started little rituals that happen every day. I picked up on this notion as I was showing Tim today around the building and nearby vicinity. Each day I say good morning to the security guard in the lobby who used to be a scout master for his son's Boy Scout troop, we've been comparing notes. I pay for my parking for the day.*

I check Austin's dry erase board daily to see what nurse and intensivist has him. We have our favorites. I get free coffee and muffins from the parent food table in the nurse's station, get a daily inspiration text from my sister-in-law Patty and from my friend Lori from church, update Mr. Ward on Austin's progress, do our Pediatric Grand Rounds at 9am, drive to nearby locations for lunch and dinners for us all, and update the hotel staff nightly now on Austin's progress. They have me show them pictures too. The pretzel restaurant staff made me take pics of Austin eating their menu items today because they felt honored that a kid was craving their food after 14 days of not eating. I have to return this week to show them the pictures. I have now been to the towns of Parsippany, Livingston, Millburn, West Orange, Orange, Union, Springfield, and Liberty. Tomorrow I add Newark since my sis flies into that airport. I've noticed that a lot of the Jersey people I've met stay in their comfort zones. When I told them about all the eating places we have grabbed food from and the places I've driven through or things I've noticed on my drives they have generally no clue of what I'm talking about. A lot of employees commute fair distances to St. Barnabas and commute back to their houses and don't notice what's in between. I am blessed in this horrible situation of not being in my comfort zones to have explored communities that I never would have been a part of. I have left menus behind at the nurse's station and shared my findings with the staff so that they can know about these places as well. They certainly have got a lot of information out about Illinois from the 3 of us. I've made sure to brag on us. LOL.....thank you for ongoing prayers.

#FykeItUp

CHAPTER 21

Blueprints for Discharge

May 3, 2018

I t was challenging getting up and ready and over to the hospital for a 7 a.m. team meeting but it was well worth it. Much to my surprise, we gathered in Austin's room for the meeting. I had a vision of a group of people in a conference room and a somewhat official family conference for the books but Barnabas has more of a patient-focused culture and they have included Austin in all the discussions to date. It was our family and our team of physicians in a circle next to Austin's bed. I also thought it would be a "hurry up and talk because people are busy" meeting but again, not the case. We sat for forty-five minutes and discussed every detail with intention. Austin got his questions answered as did David and I. My post of the morning sums it up well:

> *So your prayers continue to work.....our confer-*
> *ence with the team this morning was powerful.*
> *Much to all of our surprise, the neurosurgeon in*
> *Chicago did one of his residencies at Barnabas and*
> *knows the system up here well and a lot of people.*
> *Unbelievable! Our infectious disease doctor knows*
> *the Chicago neurosurgeon because she did one of*

her fellowships down there in Chicago working closely with him and says he is amazing and very skilled. The problem we have to work on today is how to get Austin to Chicago because he is medically too stable to have a crisis flight paid for by insurance but has to fly because of his brain risks and has to be medically monitored. So getting it paid for is what we have to figure out and they think the Chicago people will have the answers hopefully. We're stranded here until the answer evolves.

They said no restrictions on any instrument playing in the fall back at school. This is a win!! We were worried about the brass and woodwinds but not a problem. He said no marching on the field this season but playing his instrument on the sideline is fine. Helmet is on for 6 months until surgery can be done to replace the skull bone with a synthetic bone. Surgery takes about 2 hours and he would only have to stay overnight before discharge back to Decatur. Wow!! That's awesome. No driver's license until skull is fixed. Soooooo... .....a lot for Austin to digest but with your prayers, love, and support on team #FykeItUp, we can do this. The gift of keeping the saxophone and other instruments in his life is such a blessing for this kid! The rest will fall back into order with time. Stay with us a bit longer in Jersey, watch out for our Jamie as we miss him more than we can say, and pray for a transport solution to Chicago.......

#FykeItUp

Jamie was being well-looked after by the team in Mt. Zion. He had now been at his friend Nick's house for twelve days. Nick's mom, Jennifer, and I joke all the time about Jamie being her fifth son since he is there quite often, but in no way did I anticipate that he would have a "sleepover" this long at Nick's house. They take such great care of him on any other day and this was no exception. She would call me with questions about school or anything else. She even signed his permission slip to go to a St. Louis Cardinal's baseball game with his class at school. He was doing fine, and between David and I, he was getting calls frequently. I would receive messages from his teachers and other faculty at the Mt. Zion Junior High. They were keeping an eye on him and making sure that he seemed happy and adjusted to having his parents gone. I always got good reports. David and I were comforted by the idea that Jamie was surrounded by love. One of our friends had a connection with a pilot who would fly him to New Jersey to visit us briefly but he was too scared to fly on a small plane with strangers, so he declined. We completely understood. It was a lot for a twelve-year-old to take on.

Jamie at Cardinal's game

Off I went to the Newark airport to pick up my sister Lori. I enjoyed the ride because I had not been in that area while Austin had been hospitalized. The view of the skylines was excellent. I love driving near bodies of water as well and I believe the airport was near what is called Newark Bay. Lori was ready to be picked up just as soon as I pulled in. It was good to have her there. We dropped her belongings off at the hotel and headed back to Barnabas. When we got to the room, Austin and David greeted Lori and she was immediately briefed on how things were progressing and how things flow at Barnabas. While I was gone, a medical harpist had stopped by to play for Austin. I had never heard of this type of music therapy. She is part of the Pastoral Care staff at Barnabas and is certified to play music for patients in a medical setting. David shared that she had played a variety of music including Guns 'N Roses' "Sweet Child of Mine," Elvis music, "Edelweiss" from the *Sound of Music*, and more. She told David and Austin that she trains other players to be medical harpists and provides their certifications. Her harp was on a small rolling platform and stood about four feet tall. I was so sorry to have missed her playing but Austin enjoyed it and that was the goal of the music. I was just so impressed with how this hospital had adopted music therapy at the bedside. We were all reaping the benefits. I think caregivers also need ways to reduce stress while spending so much time at a hospital. I made a note in my head that I would talk about all these alternative therapies that Austin was receiving once I got back home.

Medical Harp player

We received wonderful news today from a medical air transport company named AeroCare. They would be willing to cover half the cost of a flight back to Chicago for Austin if our Blue Cross Blue Shield would pay the other half. They had been contacted by one of my friends, Sara, who works as a nurse in the Chicago area. Sara had read my posts about our medical air flight dilemma and emailed a connection she had at AeroCare to ask for their help. I received a call from their staff explaining their willingness to help and how the process happens for this type of transport. It was all so overwhelming and I was so appreciative of a company offering this option. The case manager was negotiating on our behalf and would keep us updated as she learned more details.

Pastor Kevin from Livingston United Methodist Church stopped by to see Austin that afternoon. One would think it would be awkward having a strange pastor making rounds to see you but he was awesome from the first few minutes on. We felt very comfortable talking to him. I think he spent an hour on that first visit. The amazing fact that we discovered is that Kevin had grown up in DeKalb, Illinois, which is the same town that I got my nursing degree in. I went to Northern Illinois University for my Bachelor's in nursing from 1983-1987. Kevin's father had been a librarian around that same time and was assigned to look after all the students who were majoring in the sciences, which included nursing. I remembered spending so much time at that library that I guaranteed him that his father had helped me at some point in time, maybe provided the freshman orientation of the library for us. We also figured out that he had once lived in Seattle many years ago, residing in a house that was only one block away from a house that my sister had lived in. They had missed each other by one year. Just crazy! It was just one more connection that I had encountered during our time in New Jersey.

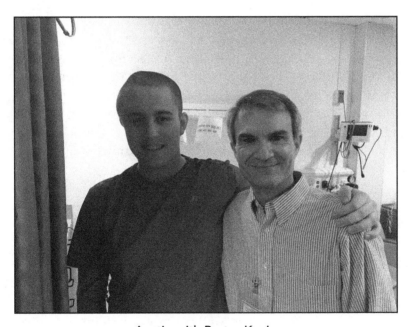

Austin with Pastor Kevin

I was really feeling like we were only two or three degrees separated from each other rather than the six degrees of separation that everyone talks about. I think you have to engage in dialogue and heartfelt conversations with people around you to understand this concept. If you spend your life avoiding people or putting headphones on during plane rides so you don't have to talk to the person next to you, I think you will miss the opportunity to discover the beauty in humanity. We all have stories that we carry around with us and yes, some of the stories aren't things we want to be disclosed. Some stories are worth forgetting or blocking out in our memories. Yet, a lot of our stories are rich in nature and would be so worth sharing with others if people would only open their hearts and minds and be willing to listen. So I find common denominators with people in so many of my conversations whether they are my friends or total strangers because I choose to listen and interact with those around me. And I was certainly finding them in New Jersey left and right. Kevin left and promised to stop by again because clearly, we enjoyed having him there.

The last visitor of the day was Melissa the music therapist again. This time, she brought her guitar and *Phantom of the Opera* guitar music. She had been practicing it all week and was ready to share it with Austin. She sang the theme song for us and it was just beautiful. Her voice was warm and her guitar playing was a great accompaniment. We were happy that she finally was able to share her gifts with us after being so patient for the past week. We asked her many questions about her role at the hospital and how she was able to make this work as a full-time position. She had to start slowly to show the worth in what she was doing for patients. Once she got her foot in the door and got established, she was able to show the benefit of music therapy and increase her weekly hours. We loved having her in our experience. She promised she would come back again and share more *Phantom* music. The rest of the day, we just visited with Aunt Lori and had pizza for dinner, which we carried out from our new favorite local restaurant, Master Pizza. We called it a night and headed back to the hotel. I was praying that the next day would give us answers about the flight to Chicago.

Melissa the Music Therapist

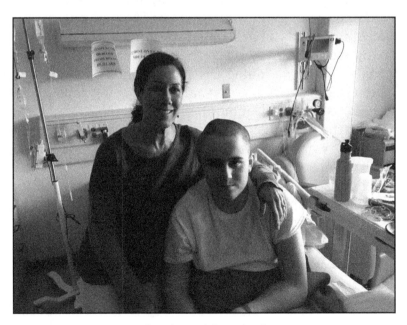

Austin and Aunt Lori

CHAPTER 22

Enter Breakfast Lady #2

May 4, 2018

This morning at breakfast we were told that our meals would be no charge because of what we were going through. I had been sharing updates with the restaurant people daily, as well as with the people at the front desk, and showing pictures from the hospital of all the pets, music therapies, and more. They were praying for Austin and asking every time we were back at the hotel how he was doing. Our favorite breakfast lady at this location was named Lexie. She had a smile that was contagious and such a sweet demeanor. She was not a Jersey native. She was from the Bahamas. I never did ask her why she moved to Jersey since we talked so much about the hospital and progress Austin was making. She expressed interest in helping us in any way she could. She said she would talk to the manager of the hotel and see if she could help us as well.

Me with Lexie

Today was a day spent arguing with Blue Cross. I spent over an hour and a half on the phone with them in the morning trying to convince them that Austin's illness was life-threatening and would need a critical care flight to Chicago for monitoring purposes. They would put me on hold about every ten minutes and come back and argue again. I felt like I was drowning in a sea of no hope. I thought to myself, "What if we are stuck here for days on end figuring this out? What if he gets denied and AeroCare really can't get us home? What if the neurosurgeon insists that flying commercial or driving the trip to Chicago in private car is not an option? What will happen if my hand is forced and we have to go by car or commercial air against medical advice?" All I knew was I would go crazy if we were stuck here, doing nothing to get out. Surely we weren't the first people to have to go through this situation. I hung up with them exhausted and went back to Austin's room. Tim was back visiting today on his way out of town, heading to Illinois. We were told that we would be moving today from the PICU department to the regular Pediatrics unit. So, Lori and Tim helped David and I move all the belongings and get settled in our new room. It wasn't as spacious but we were hoping it would be only a few short days in this room before heading to Chicago. The one positive thing is that it had a private bathroom and shower so we wouldn't have to take Austin down the hall to shower anymore and there would be a lot more privacy in this bathroom than in the PICU rooms. Our first nurse assigned to us on Peds (Pediatrics unit) was Ruth and we loved her from the start. She was a seasoned nurse of over twenty years on this Peds unit and was very comforting. The manager of the unit also stopped by to welcome us. Everyone on the team seemed to already know Austin's story, so I was reassured that the handoff between departments was done well.

We said goodbye to Tim. He promised he would be at our church back home this weekend and would share updates with the congregation. They had been praying for us from afar and sending messages routinely. We worked with the case managers of the PICU and Peds unit the rest of the afternoon trying to escalate our plight to the higher tiers within the Blue Cross empire. We were warned that we may not hear anything over the weekend and we would have to continue the discussion on Monday. Oh, wow—three more days of hurry up and wait. I was pacing the halls. Actually, I went out to the pond on the campus of the hospital and stared at the ducks. It was mindless activity because my brain was in shutdown mode. I can't describe how tiring it is arguing a point that you know to be the truth, trying to get people who make all the decisions to believe what you are saying. I had even cried to the insurance people today. I felt like I sold my soul to them and begged from a mother's perspective to please pay for his transport home.

I prayed by that pond, too. I begged God to listen to all of our prayers and please take the choke hold off of us. Upon return to the room, Lori and I decided to go to Nero's Steakhouse down the road to get dinner and bring Austin back another steak like we had done a few days ago. David decided to stay back. We ate a quick dinner on their back patio before the rains took over and we had to dash inside. The spring weather was starting to evolve and the rain and buds on the trees were starting to make appearances. Had we really been here long enough for the seasons to change? I'd say so. We dropped off Austin's dinner, visited for a bit, and then headed to the hotel.

On the drive to the hotel, I received a call from a writer from the *Herald & Review*, which is our local newspaper back home in Decatur. He had heard about Austin's story and wanted to do an interview with me for an article for the following day's paper. I consented and told him I'd call him once I was back to the hotel. I wasn't sure if someone had called him or if he had seen something about it from the GoFundMe page but I was fine with doing the interview. I spoke to him for about fifteen minutes, visited with Lori for a bit, and then wrote my post for the day. Here it is:

On April 22 I argued with the hotel staff that I wanted to drive back to Illinois. I needed my own people to take care of Austin. I didn't know anyone here and didn't want to go to a strange hospital. I even sat there in the St. Clare's ER thinking of ways to escape from the foreign land with weird speaking people who didn't know my nursing background and even less about Illinois. Everyone asked me if I was from Chicago. But when the ER doctor looks your right in the eyes and says your son is going to an even bigger "foreign hospital" and have his brain worked on within hours, you have to assimilate into the Jersey way of life.

When you are immersed in a culture for more than a few days and forced to truly live as they do, you start to gain a new insight. It's not rose colored glasses that we wear during vacations to fun spots. It's real people, treating you like locals, and expecting you to conform to society where you are in the moment. This is our streets, this is our businesses, and this is how we act. "We all know there aren't fast food restaurants everywhere but it's our choice. We eat differently in Jersey. We love our bagels and we are proud for you to try them. " I seriously had to drive a half hour to find a McDonald's on the day I just wanted a simple burger. And, several locals have brought the Fykes bags of bagels to show off their wares. Yes, proud is how I would describe Jersey folks and very robust. My sister says her East coast friends that have transplanted back home say they can be brash but would take a bullet for you. They say what they mean, and mean what they say. I've enjoyed watching locals banter about sports teams, the weather, who's wrong or right or even about small annoyances. They get annoyed easily.

The roads are crazy and built from what I heard based on horse paths of the day, lol. There are few left or right turns, it's just veer left or right. U turns are your friend and oftentimes necessary. Don't make eye contact when you fight for a parking spot or to take a lead on a merged road. Fight for everything here and don't be remorseful. It's just their way of being and they don't see each other as rude or brash. But, wow have they embraced our story and had our backs. The Jersey aggressors have made a difference in our lives. They know what I need to do sometimes when I don't know and they are not afraid to ask for forgiveness rather than ask for permission. I feel "held" up here in a weird sort of way but I would say a Jersey sort of way. I'm going to miss these people when we clear out of here and get some organization back in our lives. And they'll miss us. Austin is now known around this building as the kid that went on a band trip to New York and wound up on the Jersey side with brain surgery. They have all requested that he sends pics up here from next marching band season showing them Austin in his element. We may just come back in person someday to say hello.

#FykeItUp

As I reviewed the events of the day in my mind while trying to fall asleep I could only pray that the insurance people would come to their senses and cover the cost of our trip to Chicago.

CHAPTER 23

Please Bring Me Mexican Food

May 5, 2018

This morning at breakfast, we made sure to say hello to Lexie. She gave us free breakfast again and said the manager wanted to talk to us. She came out and sat down with Lori and me for quite a while, listening to updates on Austin and expressing her wishes for his recovery. She then proceeded to share that she would be dropping our hotel rate down to the price that employees pay when they stay within the network of their hotels. The savings were significant and I couldn't do anything else but hug her. It was such a blessing. New Jersey rates compared to those back home were very expensive and were draining the funds we had rapidly. This group of employees was just amazing the whole time we were staying at the hotel. They even gave us a card signed by all of them to give to Austin. God's work here in New Jersey....

The day was quiet since we wouldn't hear from Blue Cross on the weekend. We just visited and tried to keep Austin's spirits up. We watched the Kentucky Derby on television and all picked who we thought would win. For dinner, Austin wanted Mexican so Lori and I volunteered to head into South Orange to get food from a place we had found online. One small detail—we forgot that today was Cinco de Mayo. The staff at

94

the restaurant told us there would be no way we could get a carryout order placed and doubted anywhere in the area would be able to take our order. It's their busiest day of the year. So, we switched cultures for our culinary experience and found a small Chinese restaurant instead for dinner to take back to the hospital. It was the best we could do at the moment.

Throughout the day I had received messages from back home about Austin's story being in the *Herald & Review* newspaper. It was very well written and I was quoted correctly. Actually, the author had taken the time to add small details that I had not provided, but which were accurate and appreciated. You never know how your statements will be shared in the media but I thought he did an excellent job. The picture that they used for the article was one that my sister-in-law, Patty, had taken of Austin last November when he was participating in High School Day with the marching band at Illinois State University. That day, it had snowed heavily right in the middle of the performance and the band was having a heck of a time completing the performance. My nephew Mike was one of the drum majors at the time and Austin had shared that the snow was so heavy that no one could even see the drum majors. It was a memorable day for Austin and his friend Ethan who joined him. They had so much fun and the picture showed it by the smile on Austin's face.

Austin at Illinois State University

Once back at the hotel for the night, Lori and I were in the hotel lobby debriefing with each other when my phone rang. It was a gentleman from Decatur named Jeff. I didn't know him personally but he was calling to offer to fly up to New Jersey to pick up Austin and bring him to Chicago for us. He had heard about our struggles and was willing to help out because he owned a plane and had a pilot that could come for us. My heart sank because here was a ride home on a silver platter and we couldn't accept the offer due to needing a medical transport service. I thanked him up and down for what he was willing to do and hung up the phone. I turned to my sister and explained what the call was about and surprisingly, she recognized the name because he was a client of her husband's business. She would be sure to have him call Jeff and thank him for trying to reach out to our family. A total stranger willing to help us out to such extremes—there is so much good in the world, yet people continue to bank on headlines that showcase the bad news. In the midst of a very painful time for our family, I was beginning to see signs of goodness threaded throughout the whole experience. And I found myself thinking that maybe we should let this goodness prevail over all else; just maybe.

CHAPTER 24

It Is Well with My Soul

May 6, 2018

Because Pastor Kevin had been by to see us a couple times at Barnabas, I decided that today I would go to his place. Livingston United Methodist church was just a few minutes away and a very easy drive. I got there a few minutes early and found a seat behind a few others who had arrived early too. They were very welcoming. I knew I would be noticed as Kevin had shared that he had a small congregation of a little over forty congregants. He had quite a diverse group though, with people from over twenty different ethnic backgrounds. I sat behind a lady named Dottie, who I was guessing to be from an African country but I did not ask her specifically which one. The service was inspirational and I was invited to join them for fellowship afterward to celebrate Dottie's birthday. I graciously accepted and took up conversation with several of the members. One of the ladies gave me even more information on how Jersey people are and how the rest of the country misinterprets the Jersey way due to the shows on television. I was glad to get the input from a local versus an actor. My post for the day sums up my time at Livingston UMC:

My takeaways from church this morning:

1. *We figured out this morning that Pastor Kevin's dad was my librarian at NIU in 1983. He had the biology and nursing majors. Crazy, crazy, crazy.....and the insane hours I spent in that library!*
2. *Methodists are always feeding the world, they sent me back to the hospital with cookies for us and the Barnabas staff on Peds*
3. *Jersey people think that the rest of the country make fun of them and that they are misunderstood*
4. *That the hymn for today's service must have been planted by God for my benefit. "It is Well With My Soul" by Horatio Spafford. I was taught this past year by a couple friends why that song was written. A man lost all 5 of his children and business within such a short period of time was able to write the words to this song as a response to his hardships. It inspires me to know that this hardship in front of us can ultimately be well in my soul too......God is with us. The people of Livingston UMC were very gracious to me this morning and are now among all of us praying for Austin*

#FykeItUp

When I got back to the hospital, it was time to take Lori back to the airport. I was sad to see her go but thrilled that she got to spend a few days with Austin. She promised him she would see him in Chicago once he got to Lurie's. I dropped her off and told her that I hoped to see her sooner than later if I had my way. And then she was gone—yet another person getting to go back to Illinois. I kept thinking about that band trip bus and the two empty seats that had left a long time ago. Friends and family here for short stays and back to their lives. When would it be our turn? What is our new normal going to be? How will the summer be? Clearly, I worried and made up things in my head way too much. I needed to put my faith in God and let Him get us home. I knew He would unveil our plan soon. I was just being impatient.

We had a quiet rest of the day on the Peds unit and then David and I both headed back to the hotel since the manager had drastically dropped the room rates. We could each have our own rooms and quiet time. Austin was going to be fine and could call us for anything. He was doing well and we foresaw no reason why we had to stay at the hospital at night now. This would be a test but David was tired of sleeping in a hospital bed and needed the hotel room. Hopefully, tomorrow we would hear news on the plan.

CHAPTER 25

We're Going Home!!!

May 7, 2018

I t was a beautiful day in New Jersey this morning. I got moving early in hopes of hearing from the insurance people. Austin was craving McDonald's pancakes every morning, so I had made several trips to West Orange to satisfy his cravings. Today was yet another one of those trips. As I pulled into the hospital parking lot, I saw two helicopters marked NYPD landing on the hospital heliport pads. I had all kinds of ideas in my head on what might be happening. Of course, I thought it was either an incarcerated patient being brought in or maybe being picked up. When I got to Austin's room, David and Austin had been watching from the window and saw about six men in black suits get out of each of the helicopters and jump into black sedans and drive away. They said it was like a scene out of a movie. Who knows for sure what was going on, but it was interesting needless to say. Austin looked good and was anxious to hear about being discharged or not. We visited for a while and then, finally, our case manager casually walked into the room and told us that Blue Cross was going to pay for the ride 100% and that the flight would be from a company called AMR. They had the ability to do the transport at 10 a.m. – 11 a.m. the next day. I asked why not AeroCare and she said that Blue Cross chooses who they want when paying for the flight. She gave us information on AMR and we were fine with the information. We requested a phone call interview with a representative from their company so that we could get our questions answered. The case manager said she would set that up and have them call us later in the day. And then she left. I couldn't believe it—we had a ticket to ride. I think all three of us did a happy dance. Finally! It was such a sense of freedom and relief. I had a new-found energy level. Oh, gosh! We need to pack up! We need to load up the van with what can go to Decatur! We need to let family know what's going on—plus a thousand more worries in my head. Here was my post:

YOUR......PRAYERS......WORKED!!!!

Blue Cross Blue Shield is paying 100%!!!!! We're out of here tomorrow morning at 10am to Chicago.......Thank you!!!! God is good

#FykeItUp

We scrambled around like crazy, cleaning up the room down the hall that we had taken over for belongings and care packages and such for the past two and a half weeks. At one point in time, we took up four rooms between sleeping rooms and Austin's room and the room next to it, but it was only because their patient census was low while we were there. We always knew that if it got crowded that we would have to condense but we lucked out. And the staff in the PICU was very forgiving. We were only going to be able to pack a small bag for the flight due to weight restrictions, so here I was again, thinking about how my wardrobe was going to be slim just like on April 22. I didn't even care. I would be staying at my sister's house in Evanston, Illinois, while Austin stayed at Lurie's and I could wash clothes as needed. I was praying that we would only be there for a couple days since Austin was doing so well.

Melissa came by with her guitar that afternoon and played a song from the *Phantom* that really got me choked up. It is enti-tled "Think of Me" and it was such a perfect song for the closure to our relationship. I hate closure! I recorded her singing it to

Austin and have played it a 100 times since that day. Her voice is so beautiful and the music is so touching. She touched our hearts during our stay and we will never forget her. Music has that effect on the spirit. It's a feeling I can't explain except to know that the effect is real. Music is healing and I have seen the power of it in these past weeks. I will talk about it forever and give the biggest testimony if ever asked about why it should be a part of every patient experience as appropriate.

The AMR representative called and answered all of our questions and put us at ease that we would be in good hands. There would be a critical care nurse and respiratory therapist on the flight, as well as two pilots. They had antiepileptic medications in the kit if needed. They would monitor Austin the whole trip. We would take an ambulance off-site from the hospital to the airport in Morristown. From there, we would be flying into Midway airport in Chicago. From Midway, an ambulance would take us to Lurie's. It sounded all orchestrated and planned. I was sad that AeroCare didn't get the flight after all the negotiating they had done with Blue Cross but I will always credit nurse Sara in Chicago who reached out to AeroCare and also credit the staff at AeroCare for being the spark that lit the flame. I think that their pressure, along with my own and from the case managers pushed Blue Cross into the decision to provide full coverage. For that, I am eternally grateful and will always recommend AeroCare to others.

We tucked Austin in for the night and headed back to the hotel one last time to get some sleep before the big day. I was oddly sad that I would be leaving this place with such a warm and caring staff. They had been so good to us. It felt like home away from home. I sat in my room and reflected on the people we had met while here and shed tears thinking about saying goodbye to them. I posted pictures of some of the lifesavers and heroes from Barnabas. Whereas everyone was amazing, we still had our favorites who will always be remembered. I couldn't think of a single person on the team that we didn't care for. I would say for a family that was there for seventeen days, that's pretty good. It speaks volumes about the culture of Barnabas. I quickly packed my bag for the flight and nodded off to sleep.

CHAPTER 26

Goodbye New Jersey!
We Love You!

May 8, 2018

W
e were up early again with the need to check out of the hotel, get Austin breakfast, pick up donuts for the PICU and Pediatric departments and then get to the hospital to say goodbye to everyone. David dropped off the donuts in PICU and shared with them that we were leaving today. It was like the shot heard all over the hospital. For the next couple of hours, we had a constant stream of Barnabas staff and physicians coming to say goodbye to Austin and taking pictures with him. I had to capture all of the faces of those that had cared for him so faithfully. There were many hugs and promises to keep them posted on our progress with letters and pictures and a visit down the road once healed. I even had permission to text Dr. Hasan with progress. I would keep this in mind. The flight crew was slightly delayed and would be coming at 11 a.m. instead of 10 a.m. We didn't mind. We were enjoying visiting with our team. David would be starting the fifteen-hour trek again to get back home as soon as we left. Austin and I tried to convince him to do it in two days but he was determined to just get home. He was missing Jamie and his dog, Punch. He would get Jamie as soon as he arrived in town. He promised to stay

in touch with calls from the road. We would do the same once we arrived in Chicago.

The AMR team arrived by 11 a.m. and loaded Austin onto the stretcher with his helmet on. We said our final goodbyes, Austin hugged his dad and we traveled through Barnabas to meet the ambulance. It was a short twenty-minute ride to Morristown where the jet was waiting for us. I had the rear seat with all the luggage and gear behind me. Austin sat upright in the middle seat and the crew had the front. We watched the pilots performing their final checks before departure. It was weird being able to see inside the cockpit. My travels in small crafts had been minimal in my lifetime, so this was interesting to me. Our flight was approximately two hours and uneventful. They had attached Austin to a standard cardiac monitor for the ride and his vital signs remained insignificant. The crew looked very relaxed for the whole trip and Austin did very well. His wound site on his head looked unchanged to me when we arrived in Chicago. The pressure changes didn't seem to have any effect on him. Austin said he enjoyed the trip and was glad to be back in Illinois. We climbed out of the plane onto the tarmac at Midway and quickly used the restrooms. Austin stayed on board until the ambulance arrived. We had a fifteen-minute wait because the ambulance was waiting at the wrong private sector of the airport. During the delay, we stood on the tarmac visiting with the pilots. I gave them a brief synopsis of what our lives had been like for the past few weeks. I noticed that as the days marched, my summaries of Austin's story were becoming more challenging to keep concise. I had so many details in my mind from New Jersey that I didn't know how to respond to anyone's question anymore of "How are things going?" or "What are the updates?" For new people in our interactions, my storyline was, "We went on a band trip and never came home...." I was dreading having to start from scratch with the Chicago team at Lurie's. I prayed that all the records got transferred and that people spent time reading them. I was not in the mood to tell the story from the start. Plus, I'm in healthcare—no one has that much time to hear this story. So, I rehearsed the elevator speech in my head on how to paint this picture.

Our jet to Chicago

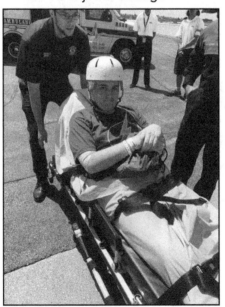

Midway airport

The ambulance ride to downtown was about thirty minutes and we found the ambulance bay easily. Our driver was worried that it would be a challenge but that was not the case. They took us to the nineteenth floor of this vast facility. We had a partial view of Lake Michigan from the window and a very nice room. The staff greeted us upon arrival and got us rapidly oriented to our surroundings. There was a big flat-screen television mounted at the foot of the bed with a "welcome Austin" message displayed. How cool! I liked Lurie's already. Shortly after our arrival, the infection control team and neurosurgery team both made rounds and spelled out the plan for Austin's stay in Chicago. These teams also had big residency groups with them. This was definitely another teaching hospital. The fantastic news of the day, however, was from our new lead neurosurgeon, Dr. DiPatri. He said he only needed Austin to stay in the hospital for a couple of days, depending on MRI results. He was going to order the MRI to be done the next day and go from there, but expected the results to be fine. More music to our ears! We were thrilled and could see light at the end of the tunnel. We called David to tell him the good news. He was going to join us in Chicago if we were going to be longer, so now he would just wait for us to come home instead. I told him I did not want him to pick us up since he would have just driven fifteen hours. I decided I would call our friend Tim again and see if he would come get us. I felt certain that he would come if he didn't have any schedule conflicts. My post for the day:

Prayer time....MRI tomorrow and if remaining frontal brain abscess shows improvement or is gone or is not concerning, then our new neurosurgeon Dr. DiPatri says home to Decatur Thursday!

IV antibiotics at home until June 16 and then maybe skull rebuild August. Skull rebuild is about a 2 hour long surgery and quick 1-2 day stay in hospital and then back to home. It will be done here at Lurie's. And, the best news of all.....he can ride by car Thursday with helmet on back to Decatur. Should have seen my reaction to that one!

Lurie Children's Hospital

#FykeItUp

Austin's Aunt Patty was planning on coming to spend the day with us tomorrow since she and my brother live in the suburbs of Chicago. Austin demanded that Patty bring him her homemade meatballs, which he had always enjoyed any time he was at her house. She promised him she would but he needed to remember that he would be nothing to eat or drink after midnight in preparation for the MRI. Austin always had to have general anesthesia for his MRIs due to claustrophobia. His test was scheduled for 2 p.m. so she would find a way to make them and keep them warm for him. He insisted that she find a way to keep them warm so he would not have to alter their taste by being microwaved later in the day. Patty and I had to giggle over this request because Austin had "meatball rules" that she had to abide by. But Patty is a people-pleaser when it comes to food so if anyone could make this work, it would be her. I gave Austin a hug and kiss goodnight and headed out of Lurie's by early evening so I could get to my sister's in Evanston

107

at a reasonable hour. I hailed an Uber ride and got there a half hour later. I visited with my sister and her family for a bit and then retired for the night. It had been a long day and I would be taking the train in the morning back downtown. But it was SO GOOD to be back in Illinois. And, whereas it was not my home, this house had been very welcoming over the years, so I was happy.

CHAPTER 27

Bring On the Meatballs

May 9, 2018

As I was getting ready this morning, I thought about how supportive the Mt. Zion School district had been throughout this ordeal. We received cards and donations from many of the teacher groups. The administrative team at the high school was making sure that all of our concerns about Austin's school year were addressed. The guidance counselor had been calling us in New Jersey and talking to Austin about how he wanted to do his coursework to finish the year. They offered him flexibility and for that, we were so thankful. Austin decided that he wanted to do as much online work as he could to bring a couple of his grades up from where they were when he left town. We actually had the Google Chromebook with us but did not have the charge cord. David and I had looked in a couple stores to get a charger for him but could not find the exact one we needed. So, Austin decided he would wait until he got home to submit the assignments. Another wonderful thing that the high school had done a couple days ago was to let all the kids pose for a picture in the bleachers by the football field and hold up a sign saying *Get Well Soon* for the kids that had recently been in the hospital. While we had been gone, there were two others who had to also seek out hospital care and the kids wanted to reach out with a special message to all of us. It really meant a lot to know they were thinking of us and many praying for healing. We would make sure to stop by the high school just as soon as we returned home and give out a personal thank you to all, plus pick up materials needed for Austin to finish his sophomore year.

I hopped on the train in Evanston to ride into the city. It is the easiest and most affordable solution for transportation needs to downtown Chicago. Patty was going to meet me near my stop and drive to the hospital parking garage. I did a lot of meditation on the train ride in. It is an easy, mindless thing to do as you look out the window and stare at all the buildings and businesses going by as the train drifts down the tracks. I guess *meditation* and *mindless* are oxymoronic words but I was in that state where you can see the buildings and hear the noise around you, while thinking about life unrelated to what your senses are picking up at the moment. Maybe I was being mindful and mindless simultaneously—a paradox. Is that possible? Here was the post I wrote while at the station waiting, and then while on the train:

> *As I sit in this metro station waiting for the train from my sister's neighborhood in Evanston down to Lurie's it makes me think about how many sets of directions that I've been part of for the past 24 hours (including what's in my mind for this ride). Directions from the Barnabas team on what to do after discharge to Lurie's, directions that our air ambulance team had to follow to the small airport in NJ on to Midway and then how to get the ground ride to Lurie's. The ambulance driver was worried about finding the ambulance bay at such a complex organization. Then there was finding our room, me finding the food locations within my surroundings for dinner, and then hailing the Uber guy who followed his technology to get me to Evanston last night. And.....to elaborate.....my*

directions to food were to "take the Tower elevators to the Sky elevators to the 2nd floor and turn right and walk in the walkway all the way over to the Northwestern campus and there you will find food!" I was nauseated at the thought of that adventure. And to my surprise I did it in a 20 minute round trip (just got Subway food) without having to ask a single soul for redirection!

Here's why I think everything went well these past hours. My thinking, my perspective. Directions were designed by people to set us up for success. Signage is key. People have worked tirelessly to get people to their goals. And people before you have tweaked processes as technology and accessibility has evolved. People before you have trialed or used the directions and made it easier for you with their feedback and actions. They have done things behind the scenes for reasons we may never know. So I followed signs, flow of people and gut instinct this morning and yesterday and have reached my short term goals. Our ambulance driver in Chicago was greeted with a huge sign that said Ambulance Bay right there near the main entrance to Lurie's. I have listened with attention to the resources who have navigated through problems that I am yet a novice to. I respect those that reach out to reassure me that I'll find my way and things will be alright. Barnabas quote by my lead physicians up there "Lurie's is a great place. You'll be in good hands and they'll get you home....."

So I've decided that we should definitely follow directions this summer with the antibiotics, use of helmet, activity restrictions, holding on driver's license, infection control, communication and appointments because those before us have deemed these necessary through research, practice, expertise, others' outcomes and yes, even medical intuition. We'll also follow directions through our faith and use God as the North Star and surely we can't go astray. We look forward to coming home soon to be with our village that has distantly prayed us through. Today will be key with the MRI. News to follow soon

#FykeItUp

When Patty and I reached Austin's room, we found him in good spirits. He was hungry but I knew that would be the case with the pending MRI. Patty had a couple of large bags with her which I really didn't pay attention to until she started putting out a truck driver buffet on the counter in Austin's room. She brought snacks, meatballs, macaroni and cheese, and more. We had enough to feed everyone in the room plus the whole nineteenth-floor staff. If you know my sister-in-law, you are nodding your head, "Yes." right now and completely understanding why we had this huge buffet. Her heart is huge as well and she has a gift for taking care of people. Austin was thrilled and counting the hours until he could be part of the feast. The meatballs had arrived! I'll be glad to share this recipe if anyone is interested. So, we spent the day visiting and inviting staff to grab lunch and snacks. Austin kept careful watch over the meatballs like a shepherd watching his flock of sheep. No one had better take too many or he would be making us hide the dish. Ha! It was kind of our joke for the day.

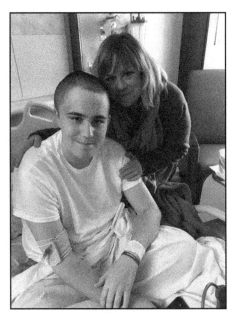

Austin and Aunt Patty

He went for the MRI as scheduled, and Patty and I took the opportunity to explore the building a bit. We grabbed coffee and found a spot on the eleventh floor where there was a few tables and chairs overlooking the city. There were panoramic windows to give us an awesome view. The signs on the wall called it a reflection space for families. We loved it and vowed to come back there to drink coffee again in September when Austin would be back for surgery. We headed back up to the room and Austin returned shortly after that asking for the meatballs, of course. We made him so happy. Meanwhile, my sister Lori joined us for another visit. We caught her up on the day's events. But the most impactful visit of the day was from Dr. DiPatri. He came up after looking at the MRI results and told Austin he was free to go home the next day! Finally! We were so excited and could hardly believe it. The MRI looked even better than the last one and he had no concerns. He would get the discharge plans started and would see us tomorrow. It was a great day! Austin called his dad and shared the good news. I hopped on the phone and called Tim and of course, he was excited to come get us. He would bring his wife Kathy and make a day of it. Our prayers had been answered yet one more time. My post:

MRI clear!!!!!! Coming home tomorrow!!!!! Boom!! Power of prayers....

#FykeItUp

We had a great visit with Lori, and by 7:30 p.m., it was time to head back to Evanston. We had said goodbye to Patty earlier and gave Austin a quick hug and kiss and headed out to get an Uber ride again. Once back at Lori's house, I organized my bag again to bring it with me on the train in the morning. I went to bed early and thought about going home as I fell asleep.

CHAPTER 28

Take Me Home Country Roads

May 10, 2018

Today's train ride was completely mindless. I just stared out the windows, thinking of nothing. Lori came back with me to the hospital. We met our brother Gary this time by our stop as he had taken the day off of work to spend with us. We parked and headed up to see Austin. Austin was doing well and was glad to see his uncle. Gary always makes Austin laugh with his sense of humor and upbeat demeanor. We had fun visiting and telling stories. Our nurse today was different than the one we had for the past two days. We had been with Ali since admission but she wasn't scheduled to come in until 3 p.m. today. We had really become connected with Ali over the short time we had been here. She was young and full of energy. She was good to Austin and made him feel he was in good hands shortly after arriving at this new place. We were hoping not to be there when she was supposed to work again but sadly, the infectious disease team wanted Austin to have his 6 p.m. IV dose of antibiotics before leaving for Decatur. I was impatient by now and just wanted to get home, as was Austin. I think he took it harder than I did. It was only a few more hours than anticipated but it felt like forever.

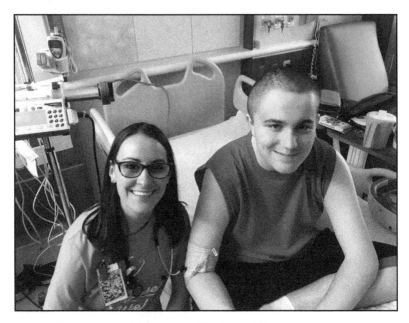

Austin with nurse Ali

Tim and Kathy were on their way up so I texted them and told them to take their time since we were stuck at the hospital for longer than I thought. They arrived and said a quick hello and then headed out to the city for the afternoon to enjoy some time together. I spent some time in the family waiting room just regrouping from my frustration of being stuck here. It was good to just sit in silence at times and tune the world out. In the midst of my sad moment, I got a message from one of my Millikin nursing students. It was a group picture of their class holding up a #FykeItUp sign and sending us well wishes. It made me smile and I asked their permission to post it because I loved it so much. They were glad to have it posted. These weren't even the students I currently had for the semester. They were from the past fall class, so I was very touched that they came together and took that picture.

Millikin University MENP nursing students

My current students whom I left on April 19, and had promised to see in a few days, had been sending me messages as well with prayers and encouragement. I felt like I had abandoned the group that I had in clinical. We were getting ready for a big presentation and winding up our semester. I was planning to sit in on their presentation through FaceTime or Skype this day but it was right in the middle of discharge planning for Austin, so I couldn't take the time to do it. I heard from many that it went well. My colleague, Jamie, graciously stepped up and covered my last five clinical days with the students and helped to facilitate their presentation. The faculty that I work with are the best and were sending me prayers and well wishes also. My director worked closely with me to come up with a plan for alleviating my summer responsibilities, which I felt I wouldn't be able to accommodate. Once again, my colleagues came to the rescue. Charlotte and Julie took on my summer load so that I could concentrate on taking care of Austin. I am blessed to be part of a great faculty and love working for Millikin.

My sister and brother left in the middle of the afternoon, so Austin and I took the time to nap and spend some quiet time together. We really didn't have anything left to do except for the antibiotic at 6 p.m. Tim and Kathy came back at about 5 p.m. and we started loading their car with bags of things needing to go home with us. Ali was back and with us for the remainder of our time at Lurie's, so we were thrilled to get to see her again. We will ask for her in September for our surgery experience. She brought the IV med in right on time and infused it over fifteen minutes.

It was finally time for the wheelchair and time to head down to the exit. FINALLY! We stopped off on the eleventh floor to show Austin the view from the reflection area and then headed all the way out of the building. Tim had pulled the car up for us. It was extremely busy outside as the business people were all bustling about and scurrying in a million directions. I don't know what came over me but I describe it as the scene in the opening credits for the Mary Tyler Moore show where she stands on a street corner (except she was in Minneapolis), and takes her hat off and throws it up in the air because she is so happy. So, I looked around at the crowd and yelled with my arms wide open and up in the air "We're going home!" They all started clapping and Austin was shaking his head like, "Mom, please...." Yes, I probably embarrassed him, but I could not help it. At last, we were going home.

Austin stopping by 11th floor Reflection Space on way out

CHAPTER 29

There's No Place like Home

May 11, 2018

The ride home the night before was smooth and filled with conversation between the four of us. We enjoyed visiting with Tim and Kathy and said goodbye to them around 11 p.m. We just threw our stuff in the house and intended to go right to sleep.

Upon entering the kitchen, I was pleasantly surprised by what Simon had done while we were gone. I found a vase of yellow roses on the table and a whole new kitchen floor coming together and almost finished. We had been trying to work on that floor for months. All the tiles had been coming up and it reminded me of a look you would find in a fraternity basement—not pretty!

He had collected donations from co-workers at the hospital on the floor he worked (also where I worked per diem), and started the remodel job. He thought he would have more time to finish it but God had a different plan for Austin. He brought him back home quicker than anyone imagined. My heart was full from the efforts and kindness of hospital colleagues.

People from many different departments had also donated funds for our family to help with medical bills and expenses. They had been sending cards and donations and adding to the

GoFundMe account—all part of the love from home that I kept referring to as my people, my village afar. I had missed them all more than they knew. I needed them so much that I was willing to jump in a rental car just to get to them. Even though I didn't get to them, they got to us. They found the pathway to us in so many ways. I hope to be able to express our gratitude so they know how impactful their actions were. I think the best way is to pay this love forward, but to also reciprocate as needed in their lives.

My top goal of the day was to get together with Jamie in any way possible. I just couldn't wait until after school so I called the junior high and asked if I could surprise him at lunchtime and they said, "Absolutely." I went to the office and made a plan to sneak into the lunch room and come up behind him and sit down with lunch that I had brought with me.

The teachers in the office decided to be my accomplices. They hid me in a back room until all the kids were in the lunchroom. Then they were going to intentionally leave Jamie's table as the last to be invited to go through the food line so I could have plenty of time. I had my friend Janine and her son, who happened to be in the office, follow behind me with a video camera. It was perfect. It felt a bit like a reality show with the camera but I'm glad I had it taped so I could see it later.

Jamie was so happy to see me, and we embraced for a quick few seconds. He is very quiet so it is hard to know what his exact sentiments were but I could tell he was happy. I sat with him for fifteen minutes while eating and then left so he could visit with his friends. I would see him again right after school. I had missed him so much and had never been away from him for this long. He did quite well being at Nick's house regardless. Those two are like brothers and rarely get tired of each other. I would need to find a way to thank this family for their help. I would come up with something.

The rest of the day was spent going through mail, unpacking, and trying to get organized. I got our dog back from Simon. He had kept Apollo for almost the whole time we were gone. Getting Austin's IV meds infused was a new routine to initiate.

I set up a center in the living room with all the supplies. The home care nurse came by and went through all the steps of PICC (peripherally inserted central catheter) care and IV administration with David and me. I was experienced in all this from working at the hospital but I wanted to make sure that there wasn't a variance in the process since we were in a home setting. It seemed about the same. The medical supply company sent a staff person to our house when we got home the previous night, around 11 p.m., to make sure we had the antibiotics and supplies we would need to get the morning dose in. We basically had a mini infirmary going but thankfully, it would just be for a couple of months or less. I knew we would get into a routine and this would all seem less overwhelming with time. Austin was taking things easy and seemed to wear out easily as he tried to move about the house. His activity level had been low at the hospitals. We would need to work on stamina and activity tolerance now. At least he was eating and that problem was resolved.

Mr. Ward stopped by to see us. It was so good to see him and catch him up on how we were doing. He already knew most of the story from his daily texting with me and seeing our posts, but making that personal connection was even better. The poor man had taken on his first year at Mt. Zion high school as the band director and look what happened on the band trip. He had nothing to worry about. We were going to be fine and he was doing a great job with the band and orchestra kids. We're thrilled to have him onboard and look forward to his direction. The next doorbell ring was a group of eight of Austin's friends who wanted to see him and welcome him home. They all crowded into his bedroom to chat and be silly. I offered them the family room but they were happy just cutting up right where they were. Austin was so happy to have them there at the moment. He did have to take a nap, however, after all the visitors were gone. He just wore out so quickly. Hopefully, this would get better. The rest of the day was low key and we were just glad to be basking in our comfort zones. Amen!

CHAPTER 30

The Summer of 2018

July 25, 2018

The summer is happening now. This is by no means the end of Austin's story. There will surely be more MRIs and CT scans and visits to Chicago with the neurosurgeon. Then, as planned, there will be the surgery to rebuild the skull. But hopefully, the bulk of the rollercoaster is over. We have no idea what to expect for recovery time but we do know that it will be much simpler this time around.

The focus for the summer has been to keep activities limited to visits with friends, eating out, going to movies, gaming at home, and continuing the pet therapy as much as possible. We contacted the local pet therapy program in town called PawPrints Ministries and they came out with two of their dogs to visit with Austin. He was thrilled since our own dog Apollo doesn't interact with him much. I got a chance to interview the owner of the business about her mission and goals. She shared that she has twenty dogs at present but more in training. The dogs are in high demand and she hopes to get more dogs in the program to keep up with the requests for their services. She said she would come back with the dogs and visit Austin again this summer any time we want. We will definitely take her up on that offer.

Austin with PawPrints Ministries dogs

I also thought about other pets to take Austin to see. There are more than dogs that serve as pet therapists. I had been to an alpaca farm a couple of years ago in Clinton, Illinois. I made an arrangement to bring Austin to visit the alpacas. The day we picked didn't work for a couple of reasons, so we are going to reschedule. The owner of the farm had read about alpacas in relation to pet therapy. She says that she sees the potential that these animals could bring to that world. She gets to see the joy firsthand when she has visitors to her farm. Austin has a good friend named Joe whose family has horses and have offered to have Austin come visit. Then, there is Kathy who has turkeys, baby chicks, and a host of other animals, and she had welcomed us as well. So, we have many places to go and people to see.

The swimming pools and water parks and amusement parks will still be there next summer when the restrictions are lifted and then Austin can resume his usual summer lifestyle. We have had many conversations with each other while doing the IV therapy, riding in a vehicle, or waiting at doctor appointments about every topic you can think of. I'm wondering how many conversations we would have had without the restrictions. I'm enjoying the time with my son and I know his dad is too. We love being with the boys. I love watching Austin and Jamie spending quality time together these past few weeks. It is the most interaction I have seen between them in years. For the most part, the interactions have been positive. I'm not sure that I'll ever see them in complete harmony since they have polar opposite personalities, but I'll take what I can get.

We have enjoyed our home care nurse Deb. She has been so easy to work with and very flexible with the schedule. We are sad to be done with the visits, but have welcomed her to visit some time to see Austin's progress. The PICC line is now out and the antibiotics stopped. We have traveled to Chicago three times now since being home for MRIs and appointments. We took Amtrak most recently as a diversion for the boys. It went very well and we may do that again.

Austin has received several care packages even after returning home. The tennis team gave him an oversized tennis ball signed by everyone, along with a gift card and sweatshirt with his name on the back. My friend Janet gave him a basket with all kinds of snacks, and another friend, Rhonda, mailed us a box with a prayer quilt from her church. Each quilt square had been prayed over for Austin. I am so amazed by all these efforts.

Austin is surrounded by prayers. He is on practically every prayer list in this area, being prayed for by his Great Banquet family; has prayers going on four continents through connections of friends; has had donations and gifts sent from Simon's parents and sister, Mary, as well as from Mary's church; and also has our whole church supporting him.

We continue to work with the Make-A-Wish team and no matter whether Austin chooses a trip to New York City or not, we will plan to return next year to try the trip all over again. And yes, we will stop by and see Breakfast Lady and St. Barnabas friends. So for now, we wait and pray for healing, and pray for the gifts God has given us in the midst of this journey and look forward to getting back to our normal routines.

CHAPTER 31

Lessons We Have Learned

One can take a catastrophic event and dissect it for the ways that it has negatively impacted life or one can look for opportunities to use the situation to make a difference. Our family has certainly discussed in detail the challenges that Austin's illness has presented but we have never looked for sympathy. We prefer prayers and acts of love.

I think these past two months have shown us mostly how people are able to come together, no matter the distance. We could be on another continent with the same problem and I am certain that we would have felt the same presence from the community back home. God's work in New Jersey, coupled with His work outside of New Jersey—mostly back home but not exclusively—showed how He works near and far. He is always with us and works in ways unimaginable. We witnessed this firsthand at the bedside. I recognized His work when I looked at the circumstances surrounding this whole story. We were put in a place with the right people at the right time with the right interventions and had all the right support.

The clear messages from this experience are to love one another unconditionally, remember to say thank you, appreciate those who serve, keep people updated so they don't have to worry, consider alternative therapies that have shown clear benefits in the research, put down the earbuds and headsets and talk to the people around you, and thank God continually for your blessings and miracles that He performs in your life. We love you all and are grateful that you are a part of our lives.

CPSIA information can be obtained
at www.ICGtesting.com
Printed in the USA
BVHW01s1430240918

528340BV00016B/739/P